Guanxi in the Western Context

Barbara Xiaoyu Wang

Guanxi in the Western Context

Intra-Firm Group Dynamics and Expatriate Adjustment

Barbara Xiaoyu Wang
Ashridge Executive Education
Hult International Business School
Berkhamsted, UK

ISBN 978-3-030-24000-4   ISBN 978-3-030-24001-1   (eBook)
https://doi.org/10.1007/978-3-030-24001-1

Cover illustration: © John Rawsterne/patternhead.com

This Palgrave Pivot imprint is published by the registered company Springer Nature Switzerland AG
The registered company address is: Gewerbestrasse 11, 6330 Cham, Switzerland

To Yuxiao, my beloved daughter.

Foreword

Barbara has seen and been part of the internationalization of China over the past decades. China has transformed from being inward looking, low-income economy to a rapidly growing externally engaged economy. Part has been the reform and opening up.

Barbara Wang has both been part of this transformation and an observer and analyst of the development of China, in particular the relationship between Western and Chinese business. As one of the early employees of a foreign business after the opening up of China from the 1980s, she saw the cultural and related challenges of China's internationalization. Working in business schools, first in China and then in the UK.

Initially focus on attracting foreign investment to boost the economy and bring in management skills. Combination of state-owned enterprises that have been modernising and becoming internationally competitive, privatization of some previously state-owned companies, entrepreneurial local government and new start-ups have given a new structure. Transformation of Shenzhen in two phases—from rural to manufacturing, and from manufacturing to technology and services. The global growth of Chinese companies is a phenomenon.

At the same time, Chinese culture has changed but much more slowly. There is still much greater respect for age and hierarchy than in the West. The orientation towards the group rather than individualism may have reduced and focuses more on the family, but is still a key feature of society. Face (*mianzi*, 面子) is still a very important consideration in everyday life and at work where criticism in public is taken very seriously. Guanxi (关系), often translated as "relationships", is a key feature and the topic of this insightful book.

As Barbara Wang makes clear, guanxi is pervasive in Chinese culture, spanning personal and work dimensions in contrast to Western relationships that are typically *either* personal *or* work-related. They are long-lasting and less focused on short-term reciprocity. Yet, they are in many ways transactional. This complexity makes guanxi difficult for many Westerners to understand and to practice effectively with Chinese counterparts.

Ningbo, China

Professor Martin Lockett
Dean, Faculty of Business, Nottingham
University Business School China

Preface

The degree of social, political, business, and cultural change in China in the past three decades is completely unprecedented and beyond anyone's expectations. My 20 years' practical experience in Western multinational companies (MNCs) in China and eight years' teaching in the UK triggered me to embark upon the pursuit of a Ph.D. in order to satisfy my pressing need to explore how Chinese and Westerners could appreciate each other and work together without unnecessary conflicts or compromising their own values, given my witnessing of numerous failures in international business due to the misconceptions and differences that appear when West meets East. In particular, frustrations have commonly arisen, when doing business across cultures, from both my Chinese and my Western colleagues, who are mainly senior managers working for MNCs. Among all the "Chinese myths", the guanxi phenomenon likely ranks the highest because it is pervasive and entrenched in Chinese society, and yet, it puzzles Westerners. Guanxi is such a powerful thing to which the Chinese are addicted, with its attachments of "love and hate". It is simply a part of Chinese DNA. Having been perceived to be a "Westernised Chinese", I cannot name a single success in either my professional or private life without guanxi elements in it. In my eight years of living and working in the UK, I have been through ups and downs during which I was doing guanxi practice and guanxi building with both host-country nationals (HCNs) and host-country Chinese (HCC). Eventually, I formed my guanxi circle, consisting of both Chinese and Westerners. Subsequently, these four years of Ph.D. research would not have been accomplished without guanxi to access informants willing to share their true feelings and thoughts. In other words, this book represents the labour of my guanxi practice and building in the West. It was challenging but by all means worthwhile.

Two and a half decades is probably a long enough time in which to depict one's working life. However, this is not true in my case. I belong to a generation that bridged those preceding it and struck out on my own, and can therefore claim many "firsts" since China reopened and reformed in 1978: the first generation to have proper academic education after the Cultural Revolution (1966–1976); the first cohort of students to have studied the English language; the first batch of Chinese employees to have worked at Western MNCs in China; the first echelon of Chinese managers to take over from expatriates and thus to localize Western MNCs. My entire career history can therefore act as an empirical study of a generation who witnessed and experienced drastic changes in international business and who transformed Western MNCs into "glocal" organizations in China and enabled Chinese MNCs to successfully operate in the West.

My Journey

1990s: The First Person to Try a Tomato. Owing to my growing up in a "business colony", I am considered to be one of the Westernised mainland Chinese managers working for Western MNCs. Born in Beijing in 1969 as the elder child of two, I am a member of the "In-Between Generation". By the time, I started my primary school education in the spring of 1977, it was the first year that academic education had resumed since the end of the Cultural Revolution. The only thing I can remember about my first day at school is how all the teachers kept saying, "What a lucky girl you are". When I graduated in 1991, I was one of a few "rebellious" graduates who decided not to pursue a position in government or at a state-owned enterprise (SOE), but, against my father's wishes, instead opted for a role at a "colony" (capitalist) foreign entity. From my parents' point of view, "working for a capitalist" was immoral and unethical. Furthermore, "doing business" was degrading given that my father is a Confucian scholar as well as a role model for Communist Party members, despite being sent to the countryside for "re-education" during the Cultural Revolution. It also did not make much difference that my mother was a doctor in Western medicine who had graduated from a school established by a German. Both of them completed their higher education before the Cultural Revolution in 1966. We are actually one of the few lucky families in modern China in which no one missed out on a proper education (either academically or culturally).

Eventually, and without informing my parents, I managed to pass the tough entry test and embark on my career in a Western MNC as one of the first batches of graduates working for Westerners. In 1991, at the age of 22, I earned more than the combined income of my parents—who both enjoyed a top salary while working in Chinese government roles—and 10 times that of my classmates who worked for the government or SOEs. My parents did not know which company I worked for until the day my German boss invited them for dinner to show his appreciation for my hard work. It was probably the first time that my parents encountered a "capitalist" in the new China. Fortunately, they were satisfied enough to support my career in the "colony" ever since. However, I did not dare tell them how "generous" the capitalist was at that time. I was worried that they might feel uneasy and consider it unfair, given that they were conditioned with the Chinese tradition of "income based on seniority".

1995: Growing Pains. Given the 50/50 joint venture (JV) formation of the Western MNC, as well as its differing cultural values and business concepts, the tensions between the two governing parties increased every day in the JV where I worked. I cannot remember how many arguments and disagreements I had to witness in the boardroom, or where I had to participate by acting as a translator. I was once almost fired by the Chinese chairman because my translation of the report written by my foreign boss was considered rude, even though I had tried hard to be as subtle as I could. Oftentimes, I had to mediate the conflicts between expatriates and local employees, which were mainly due to cultural differences and the insensitivity of Western expatriates towards Chinese protocols. I was lucky that my boss made generous efforts towards my personal development. Given that I come from a family of strong Confucian values as well as a rigid and strict Chinese education emphasizing hierarchical and authoritative status, I was liberated by and flourished within the Western management style, which is democratic and less hierarchical and authoritative. It was challenging and exciting, and I can say that I was happy most of the time. I was the first Chinese mainland manager to frequently travel internationally; I enjoyed the challenge and was sometimes overwhelmed by the responsibility and the sophistication I had to bear at the age of 26.

When I attended the Asia-Pacific Global Accounts Management Conference in Hong Kong, I saw how far Mainland China lagged behind Western countries, not to mention Hong Kong, Taiwan, Japan, Korea, and even the Philippines and Malaysia. Of all my peers, I was the youngest and most inexperienced global accounts manager. I embarrassed my Japanese colleague enormously; he was probably my father's age and thought I was the "young tea lady" before I sat next to him in the meeting room. He never got over it. However, like China, I was forced to grow up rapidly.

Numerous joint ventures emerged in China during the 1990s. However, although many of them made significant profits, they all struggled with internal conflicts between foreign and Chinese parties. The foreign parties wanted cheap labour, access to local markets and high profits; Chinese parties wanted intellectual property and technology. However, from management's point of view, the main issue was cross-cultural understanding and communication. I always considered myself the bridge, but sometimes the gap was just too wide for me to span. I once attended a board meeting to help with translation, when the British board director said, "I would like to challenge you on…" to the Chinese board director. I hesitated for a second and translated his words exactly into Chinese. When the Chinese board director heard the word "challenge", he stood up and left in a huff. His British counterpart was shocked, and I myself was stunned. The British board director looked at me and asked, "What the hell did you say to him?" "Sorry, I just repeated what you said in Chinese", I replied. In my mind I asked, "Why were you so aggressive toward the Chinese board director?" Both of us were puzzled. Actually, it took me a while to understand that the word "challenge" in the English business context is neutral and is used to discuss a difference of opinion; however, in Chinese, "challenge" is a strongly charged word, implying provocation, aggression and battle. The Chinese language is probably the most ambiguous and symbolic of all languages. A word is either positive or negative; it is very hard to find any neutral words. Furthermore, the Chinese manner of communication is highly contextual, which makes things even more complicated— even between Chinese. We often misunderstand each other with the use of certain words or tones.

2000: Great Expectations. I learned so much from my Western bosses and colleagues during my daily work. But I still wanted to know what lay behind Western management practices. When I gained my MBA from a US university in 2000, I was one of the first mainland Chinese graduates to do so; at the time, MBAs were still largely unheard of in China. Despite working in a renowned Western MNC in a senior managerial role, I was determined to undertake executive education (the education of working adults) throughout the rest of my career. Executive education was still in its infancy in China in 2000. Since then, I have journeyed into the academic world, joining the Sino-British Management Institute in Beijing in 2002; I then became a trainer and tutor, developing and delivering training and educational programmes aimed at Chinese managers working at Western MNCs.

2005: A Tale of Two Cities. It was around this time that Western MNCs lost their favoured status. Moreover, along with the steady and drastic growth of the Chinese economy, as well as China's entry into the World Trade Organisation, Chinese MNCs were now ready to prosper. With its 1 million employees, Sinopec was the largest of the top 100 SOEs in terms of size. It also had an ambitious globalization strategy. However, its biggest challenge was developing a global and strategic mindset among senior managers in order for them to execute their corporate strategy. I introduced Ashridge Business School to Sinopec, and it has sent 25 senior managers for eight weeks of training at Ashridge every year since 2005. As the programme director and a key member of the faculty, I started my journey from China to the UK in 2005.

2011: Against the Tide. At the time of the 2008 Beijing Olympics and the 2010 Shanghai Expo, the Chinese economy was in full bloom—just next to the USA. Chinese MNCs began "going out" to recruit foreigners in the West, and Western-based Chinese started "coming back" to work in China for native companies. In the fight for talent, Chinese MNCs offered much more attractive packages than Western MNCs. Somehow, I was swimming against the tide again; in 2011, while my Chinese peers were returning to China or moving to Chinese companies for better opportunities and pay, I was "rebellious" again in deciding to teach full-time at Ashridge Business School in the UK. Now, it is time for me to bridge the West and the Chinese in a different way. Fundamentally, education is at the very heart of Confucianism. As the daughter of a Confucian scholar, while I am away from my country, I feel like I am walking towards my roots, as, in contrast to its rapid economic growth, China is in desperate need of improvements to its academic and cultural education. I now work in a capitalist country, rather than just for a capitalist. However, my father seems a bit happier that I am on the "right track" as an academic, not a businessperson.

My four years of Ph.D. study have been vital to me. Having worked in the "real" world for 27 years and travelled between the "real" and "cognitive" worlds over the past four years, I have transformed from a "Westernised Chinese woman" to a "borderless human", embarking on a journey to discover a better way for people from various countries and cultures to live and work together. Confucius said, "At 40, I came to be free from doubts". In my late 40s, I definitely came to be free from doubt about cultural and social compatibilities between China and the West; this book will be worth the effort if it can do the same to the audience.

Berkhamsted, UK   Barbara Xiaoyu Wang

Acknowledgements

I would like to express my sincere gratitude to Qing Yang, the director of Bank of China London Training Centre, for providing me the opportunity and resources to carry out my research project.

It gives me immense pleasure to thank my mentor and Ph.D. supervisor Professor Davide Ravasi, for his support, guidance, reassurance, and meticulous review of my work, and for taking me through the entire journey.

I am very grateful for my friends Dave Edye, Paul Pinnington, Stephan Schubert, and Jack Sun for their constant patience, encouragement, and caring in my ups and downs during my studies.

Finally, I would like to express a deep sense of gratitude to my parents, from whom I have inherited the spirit of true intellectuals, that is, to endure self-cultivation and reflection academically, and culturally to produce knowledge and insight for social progress. Special thanks are due to my one and only loving sister Tian Wang, who always supports and stands by me in all situations. My heartful thanks to my only daughter Yuxiao, who has not only a working mother but also a studying one. She is unbelievably sensible, supportive, and loving. I love her so much!

Contents

Abbreviations

CE	Chinese Expatriate
DMA	Differential Mode of Association
FCR	Five Classified Relationships
HCC	Host-Country Chinese
HCN	Host-Country National
IA	International Assignment
JV	Joint Venture
MNC	Multinational Company
SOE	State-Owned Enterprise

List of Figures

List of Tables

1

Introduction

Abstract This chapter overviews the entire book by including personal motivation, the timely need for both China and the West. It discusses the purpose and main aspects of guanxi research, describes the structure and research focus of each chapter.

Keywords "Invisible hand" · Guanxi · Dynamics of guanxi

This book was motivated by the increasing globalization of Chinese multi-national companies (MNCs), which has had a significant impact on European economies and society. In 2016, according to Mitchell, Chazan, and Weinland (2017), Chinese investment in Europe reached a record €35.1bn, an amount four times greater than the investment by European companies in China. The rising economic and political power of China has created great interest in Chinese business practices in the West. Since the beginning of the twenty-first century, the surging globalization of Chinese firms has inspired numerous studies on the social and cultural challenges that are faced during the internationalization of firms from developing countries to the West (Boisot & Meyer, 2008; Buckley, Cross, Tan, Xin, & Voss, 2008; Child & Marinova, 2014; Child & Rodrigues,

© The Author(s) 2019
B. X. Wang, *Guanxi in the Western Context*,
https://doi.org/10.1007/978-3-030-24001-1_1

2005; Child & Tse, 2001; Cooke, 2012). In particular, Zhou, Wu, and Luo (2007) noted that some Chinese investments and mergers and acquisitions in Europe failed because of internal management challenges arising from the relationship between Chinese management and local employees, and they argued that guanxi mediated the relationship between inward and outward internationalization and firm performance.

Guanxi is widely accepted in academia as an indigenous construct from China, deeply rooted in Chinese culture, and reflected in the behaviour of Chinese people. According to a widely accepted definition, guanxi is "the closeness of a relationship that is associated with a particular set of differentiated behavioural obligations based on social and ethical norms" (Mao, Peng, & Wong, 2012, p. 1143).

The conceptualization of guanxi originates from the Five Classified Relationships (FCR, Wulun) by Confucius (Farh, Tsui, Xin, & Cheng, 1998; Wang & Rowley, 2016; Wong & Huang, 2015; Yao, Arrowsmith, & Thorn, 2016). It is articulated by Mencius (2004) (372–289 BC), the principal interpreter of Confucianism who is often described as the "second sage" after only Confucius himself,

> When it is clear that those in authority understand, human moral relationships, the people will be affectionate…Human moral relationships: love between father and son, duty between ruler and subject, distinction between husband and wife, precedence of the old over the young, and trust between friends. （人伦明于上, 小民亲于下……父子有亲, 君臣有义, 夫妇有别, 长幼有叙, 朋友有信。）

The human moral relationship, that is, guanxi, is classified in accordance with the hierarchy of social status, which carries moral values such as obligation, reciprocity, and affection. Confucius took as his highest ideal a society of people living in moral harmony, which, rather than the legal system, is the basis for peace in society (Lin, 1938). Guanxi has therefore guided the social behaviour of the Chinese for more than two millennia (Chen, Chen, & Huang, 2013; McNally, 2011; Zhang & Zhang, 2006), inducing the eminent Sinologue Lin Yutang (1938) to remark that the thoughts of Confucius were as vital in Lin's own time as they had been 2500 years ago. Building on these ideas, guanxi is defined in this book as the hierarchical human moral relationship derived from Confucian ethics for the purpose of reciprocity, obligations, and the mutual benefit of all actors in the inner circle. It is based on social and ethical norms and is the "invisible hand" that steers and synchronizes the political, economic, and social systems of China (Wang & Rowley, 2016).

Some studies (McNally, 2011; Tong, 2014) concluded that the practice of guanxi has prevailed in Chinese businesses largely because of the weak institutional system in China. However, Chen and Easterby-Smith's (2008) study on Taiwanese MNCs revealed that, although Taiwan benefited from legal institutions because of its earlier integration into the international economy through extensive American and Japanese investment, guanxi remains crucial to Taiwanese MNCs even as they become increasingly internationalized, with employees in host countries. There have been studies of guanxi at both the individual and the organizational levels (Chen, Eberly, Chiang, Farh, & Cheng, 2014). However, these studies have mainly been conducted in China. My study is one of the first to explore the indigenous Chinese guanxi in the Western context.

Although the ideology of the Chinese Communist Party towards business is derived from Marxism, and Confucianism was vilified during the Cultural Revolution of the 1960s (Zhang & Schwartz, 1997), over past two millennia, Confucian values created Chinese culture and psychology that became part of Chinese DNA, they exist and reflect at all aspects in Chinese people's life regardless of any revolutions and social change. Guanxi, one of core values, is carried by all Chinese either consciously or unconsciously wherever they go. Since mainland China reopened to the world in the 1980s, Chinese business community has evolved to three types of organization where guanxi has been practised by Chinese managers in various degrees: (1) State-owned enterprise (SOE), tightly controlled and led by central government, with the chairman or CEO also serving as an official. At the surface level, people interact each other with communist party-oriented institutional formality, and at the practical level, people get things done through guanxi practice; (2) Western MNCs and Joint Ventures (JVs), managed by Western executives, there is more Western social networking across entire organization; guanxi practice is limited in Chinese employees; and (3) Chinese private companies, dominated by family members and inner-circle friends, guanxi practice plays the key role in all activities in organization. Guanxi practice has been studied intensively in Chinese private companies; therefore, this book focuses on guanxi practice at SOEs where guanxi practice is in their recessive culture however powerful and widely implemented, especially, SOEs are the major force of globalization of Chinese MNCs in Europe.

Overview of Book

On the basis of their integrated review of research on guanxi, Chen et al. (2013) concluded that guanxi tends to be a mixture of family and non-family, personal and impersonal, and expressive and instrumental characteristics. The word guanxi, according to them, reflects the richness, flexibility, and complexity of the Chinese language. This richness is reflected in the three main aspects of guanxi examined by past research: the basis of guanxi (pre-existing particularistic ties between two interacting parties), the quality of guanxi (different levels of trust, interdependence and obligation between parties with guanxi and parties without, or between strong and weak guanxi), and the dynamics of guanxi (strategies, practices, and processes).

This book focuses on the dynamics of guanxi, which are explored in two empirical papers (Chapters 3 and 4).

Chapter 2, **Contextualisation of Guanxi**, discusses the origin and fundamental role of guanxi in China through its conceptual development, based on previous studies. In this chapter, I address the important role that guanxi plays in the Chinese socio-economic system, elaborate the notion of "Five Classified Relationships" (Wulun) of Confucian ethics, differential mode of association (chaxugeju) theory and relevant terms in guanxi study such as guanxi holder, guanxi circle, guanxi knot, and guanxi web. These ideas illustrate the fundamental role of guanxi as the "invisible hand" shaping the Chinese culture and society.

Chapter 3, **Guanxi Practices in Intra-firm Multicultural Groups: A Case of Chinese MNCs Operating in Europe**, draws, by contrast, on an empirical study exploring intra-company guanxi practices in multicultural groups outside China. Guanxi practices are understood here as the use of these social relationships to make exchanges and accomplish tasks

(Guthrie, 1998). This chapter is based on an exploratory case study that follows a qualitative approach, given that little is known about guanxi practice in a multicultural context. I selected a large Chinese MNC (BY) as a case company, and studied six of its subsidiaries, located in France, Germany, Luxemburg, the Netherlands, Portugal, and the UK, which represent cultural and institutional diversity. Many scholars studied how guanxi plays a key role in China's cultural, social, and political environment. Less is known, however, about how the employees of Chinese MNCs employ guanxi in the West. In contrast to the common assumption that all Chinese people tend to use guanxi to handle social relationships, this study reveals that while Chinese expatriates (CEs) actively practise guanxi with their homeland counterparts, they do not do so with host-country nationals (HCNs) and host-country Chinese (HCC); no such activities were observed between the last two groups. The emergent model describes how the practice of guanxi affects intra-firm multicultural group dynamics through the process of out-group activation, the formation of a superordinate group, and in-group prototyping.

Chapter 4, **Developing Guanxi in the West: Chinese Expatriates' Adjustment in Europe**, is a second empirical paper examining, in Chinese MNCs operating outside China, the building of extra-company guanxi in the process of establishing trust between parties (Chen & Chen, 2004). I employed a qualitative approach by conducting 25 semi-structured in-depth interviews in the informants' native language, Mandarin, each lasting between 40 and 90 minutes, and analysing the data through grounded theory building by coding to develop ideas, concepts, and themes. As China's global presence continues to grow, CEs have increasingly taken up international assignments (IAs) around the world. Research on how expatriates adjust to their assignments, however, has overwhelmingly been conducted on Western expatriates, and its applicability to CEs remains unclear. This chapter examines how CEs in five European subsidiaries of a large Chinese MNC develop and use guanxi in their host countries, and how this affects their adjustment. This chapter differs from the previous one because it focuses on the building of extra-company guanxi in Chinese multinationals, whereas the previous one examines intra-company guanxi practices.

Chapter 5, **Cross-Cultural Guanxi Leadership**, building on previous analysis, this chapter examines Chinese leadership in order to reveal the features of China's management system embedded deeply in its cultural—social–political environment and suggests guanxi leadership for Chinese CEs to effectively influence in foreign branches by reviewing paternalistic leadership, IAs of Chinese expatriates, and discussing the cultural intelligence (CI). Therefore, develops a conceptual framework of cross-cultural guanxi leadership and the model of cross-cultural guanxi practice for the benefit of all parties involved in working in or with Chinese MNCs.

Taken together, the six chapters explore the origin of the indigenous Chinese guanxi and its dominant role in forming the social and institutional system in Chinese MNCs. The chapters consider how, during globalization, guanxi has been practised and developed in a Western context, as well as its impact on intra-firm multicultural group dynamics and the adjustment of CEs provide effectively influencing tool, i.e. cross-cultural guanxi practising to lead cross-cultural teams.

References

Boisot, M., & Meyer, M. W. (2008). Which way through the open door? Reflections on the internationalization of Chinese firms. *Management and Organisation Review, 4*, 349–365.

Buckley, P., Cross, A., Tan, H., Xin, L., & Voss, H. (2008). Historic and emergent trends in Chinese outward direct investment. *Management International Review, 48*, 715–748.

Chen, C. C., Chen, X.-P., & Huang, S. (2013). Chinese guanxi: An integrative review and new directions for future research [中国人的关系: 综合文献回顾及未来研究方向']. *Management and Organisation Review, 9*(1), 167–207.

Chen, I. C. L., & Easterby-Smith, M. (2008). Is guanxi still working, while Chinese MNCs go global? The case of Taiwanese MNCs in the UK. *Human Systems Management, 27*(2), 131–142.

Chen, X.-P., & Chen, C. C. (2004). On the intricacies of the Chinese guanxi: A process model of guanxi development. *Asia Pacific Journal of Management, 21*(3), 305–324.

Chen, X.-P., Eberly, M. B., Chiang, T. J., Farh, J. L., & Cheng, B. S. (2014). Affective trust in Chinese leaders: Linking paternalistic leadership to employee performance. *Journal of Management, 40*(3), 796–819.

Child, J., & Marinova, S. (2014). The role of contextual combinations in the globalisation of Chinese firms. *Management and Organisation Review, 10*(3), 347–371.

Child, J., & Rodrigues, S. B. (2005). The internationalization of Chinese firms: A case for theoretical extension? *Management and Organisation Review, 1,* 381–410.

Child, J., & Tse, D. (2001). China's transition and its implications for international business. *The Journal of International Business Studies, 32*(1), 5–21.

Cooke, F. L. (2012). The globalisation of Chinese telecom corporations: Strategy, challenges and HR implications for the MNCs and host countries. *The International Journal of Human Resource Management, 23*(9), 1832–1852.

Farh, J. L., Tsui, X. K., Xin, K., & Cheng, B. S. (1998). The influence of relational demography and guanxi: The Chinese case. *Organisation Science, 9*(4), 471–488.

Guthrie, D. (1998). The declining significance of guanxi in China's economic transition. *The China Quarterly, 154,* 254–282.

Lin, Y. (1938). *The wisdom of Confucius.* New York, NY: Random House.

Mao, Y., Peng, K. Z., & Wong, C. S. (2012). Indigenous research on Asia: In search of the emic components of guanxi. *Asia Pacific Journal of Management, 29*(4), 1143–1168.

McNally, C. A. (2011). *China's changing guanxi capitalism: Private entrepreneurs between Leninist control and relentless accumulation.* Berkeley, CA: Berkeley Electronic Press.

Mencius. (2004). *Mencius.* London: Penguin Classics.

Mitchell, T., Chazan, G., & Weinland, D. (2017, January 10). Chinese investment in EU dwarfs flow the other way. *Financial Times.*

Tong, C. K. (2014). *Chinese business: Rethinking guanxi and trust in Chinese business networks.* London and New York: Springer.

Wang, B. X., & Rowley, C. (2016). Business networks and the emergence of guanxi capitalism in China: The role of the 'invisible hand'. In J. Nolan, C. Rowley, & M. Warner (Eds.), *Business networks in East Asian capitalisms* (pp. 93–118). London: Elsevier.

Wong, M., & Huang, P. (2015, July). Culturally embedded mechanism, guanxi in marketing. *Open Journal of Open Science, 3*(7), 154–158.

Yao, C., Arrowsmith, J., & Thorn, K. (2016). Exploring motivations in Chinese corporate expatriation through the lens of Confucianism. *Asia Pacific Journal of Human Resources, 54*(3), 312–331.

Zhang, T., & Schwartz, B. (1997). Confucius and the cultural revolution: A study in collective memory. *International Journal of Politics, Culture and Society, 11*(2), 189–212.

Zhang, Y., & Zhang, Z. (2006). Guanxi and organizational dynamics in China: A link between individual and organizational levels. *Journal of Business Ethics, 67*(4), 375–392.

Zhou, L., Wu, W., & Luo, X. (2007). Internationalization and the performance of born-global SMEs. *Journal of International Business Studies, 38,* 673–690.

2

Conceptualization of Guanxi

Abstract This chapter discusses the origin and fundamental role of guanxi in China through its conceptual development based on previous studies, addresses the important role that guanxi plays in the Chinese socioeconomic system, elaborates the notion of "Five Classified Relationships" (FCR) (Wulun) of Confucian ethics, differential mode of association (chaxugeju) theory and key terms in guanxi study. These ideas illustrate the fundamental role of guanxi as the "invisible hand" shaping the Chinese culture and society.

Keywords Five Classified Relationships (FCR) · Guanxi holder · Guanxi circle · Guanxi knot and guanxi web

Introduction

Guanxi is a form of Chinese concept of social networks theory; nevertheless, it has distinctive connotation and conception. The word guanxi reflects the richness, flexibility, and complexity of the Chinese language; the plethora of implicit and explicit definitions of guanxi challenges

© The Author(s) 2019
B. X. Wang, *Guanxi in the Western Context*,
https://doi.org/10.1007/978-3-030-24001-1_2

researchers (Chen, Chen, & Huang, 2013). Mao, Peng, and Wong (2012) defined guanxi as "the closeness of a relationship that is associated with a particular set of differentiated behavioural obligations based on social and ethical norms" (p. 1143). As elucidated in my co-authored paper (Wang & Rowley, 2016), guanxi is the "invisible hand" that steers and synchronizes the political, economic, and social systems in China through the hierarchical guanxi web. This web is woven by guanxi holders, who stand at the centre of guanxi circles produced by their own social influence, to serve their self-interest and the mutual benefit of all actors in the circle.

In the Confucian ethics, the "rule of man" rather than the "rule of law" is common business practice for Chinese firms. Hence, guanxi rather than law constructs the institutional domain to allow the decision making through complex social processes. Confucian harmonious society is anchored by regulated families, where each member obey to the rule of the Five Classified Relationships (FCR) (Wulun, 五伦), which are those guanxi between: (1) ruler and subject, (2) father and son, (3) elder and younger brother, (4) husband and wife, and (5) friend and friend. The Confucian vision of ideal guanxi in FCR includes a monarch's benevolence and officials' loyalty, a father's kindness and a son's filial piety, an elder brother's friendliness and the younger ones' respect, a husband's rectitude and a wife's tenderness (君仁臣忠，父慈子孝，兄友弟顺，夫义妻柔) (Zhou & Long, 2005).

A century ago, Chinese sinologist Ku Hung Ming explicated the ideal goal which Chinese civilisation sets, 'The moral obligation is the fundamental basis of social order, it is not infinite happiness for everybody, but the complete and perfect realisation of true moral being and moral order in mankind; so that the universe shall become a cosmos and all things can attain their full growth and development' (Ku, 2012, p. 10). This is the essence of Confucian 'Zhongyong', which interpreted by Ku 'The Conduct of Life' and 'The universal standard of right' (Ku, 2012). Therefore, there is a moral obligation between guanxi holders, and the relationship is mutual rather than separate. The core of reciprocation is mutual benefit, and it is the basis of guanxi (Yang, 1988).

The guanxi construct has been at the centre of a heated debate in the field during recent years. Some argue that guanxi is fundamentally different from social networks in the West and that it is a phenomenon unique to Chinese culture (Hung, 2004; Lin, 2001; Vanhonacker, 2004). Others equate guanxi with practices that are referred to as "networking" in the West (Wellman, Chen, & Dong, 2001). According to Child (2009), guanxi can also be compared with Brazilian jeitinho, Hungarian uram batyam, Russian blat, American "good old boy" networks, Japanese wa, Korean inhwa, and the Arab world's wasta. Those scholars pointed out the similarities in these concepts from other cultures, such as the importance of familial and personal relationships, in-group and out-group distinctions, and the exchange of favours. Interestingly, while guanxi tends to have neutral or even positive connotations in China, wasta in the Arab world and blat in Russia have a negative connotation (Chen et al., 2013).

Some studies (Dunfee & Warren, 2001; McNally, 2011; Tong, 2014) have argued that guanxi practice has prevailed in Chinese business mainly due to the weak institutional system in China. Dunning and Kim (2007) argued that guanxi is often an alternative to formal institutions—a sort of compensation for inadequate formal incentive structures or enforcement mechanisms. Under weak formal institutions, personal connections and networking become underlying parts of economic and social exchanges. Though informal relationships and networking are also important in the West, their role is often overshadowed by formal institutions and enforcement mechanisms (Yeung & Tung, 1996). Liu (2016) indicated that maintaining guanxi is a way for Chinese to grow a sense of security, especially in an unpredictable workplace (Wang, 2012).

Guanxi vs. Social Networks

Chen et al. (2013) argued that guanxi is a distinct research domain that incorporates social network research, leader–member exchange, and relationship making at all levels; however, dyadic guanxi relationships may serve as building blocks of a social network and go beyond the network, and the dynamics of personal exchanges may emerge inside or outside the social network.

Burt and Burzynska's (2017) social network research with 13,780 American managers and 4464 Chinese entrepreneurs provides further support to this idea. Their findings highlight similarities and differences in the way that basic network mechanisms operate in China versus the West. Based on these findings, the two researchers proposed that guanxi ties allow networks in China to operate in ways that are different from networks in the West, not because they are different in theory but because they are different in composition. This is not to say that no relational forms and practices exist in the West that closely resemble guanxi, but that the prevailing ones, as conceptualized in Western network theory, tend to be different.

According to their findings, when distinguishing guanxi from social networks, trust to some extent is high and relatively independent of social structure around the relationship. They observed that guanxi existed in those who have worked together for two or more years. They also identified that less than a tenth of manager relationships in America qualify as guanxi, and two-thirds of the Chinese entrepreneurs' key contacts qualify as guanxi, a significant difference even if the comparison between managers and entrepreneurs, on the other side, is not really a "like for like". They further found that there is no difference in terms of the amount of using connections between people with large, open networks and those limited to small, closed networks (i.e. guanxi). Thus, the purpose of guanxi practice is more specific and clearer than that of networking in terms of achieving a personal goal or favour. How many people you can connect with might be quite important for social networking, yet whom you do connect with is crucial for guanxi practice. In a nutshell, social networking is a "number game", and guanxi practice is a "member game".

According to Wang and Rowley (2016), guanxi has been one of the most crucial elements of Chinese culture and remains relevant, although the "dark side" (corruption-related) of guanxi has been acknowledged. It is deeply embedded in Chinese business organizational system given its cultural–social–political environment of mainland China. Confucian FCR constituted the basic norms of guanxi, and Chinese Sociologist Fei Xiaotong (1992) illustrated the extension of guanxi from the kinship system conceptualized Differentiation Model of Association (DMA, Chaxugeju).

The concept of DMA distinguishes Chinese social structure from Western "organisational mode of association" (Tuantigeju, Fei, 1992) that families in the West are organizations with distinct boundaries. However, in the Chinese families, everyone stands at the centre of the circles created by his or her own social influence. All circles are interrelated. In Chinese society, the networks woven by marriage and reproduction can be extended to include countless numbers of people who are from the past, present, and future (Fei, 1992). Hence, this social structure created the "egocentrism but not individualism" (Fei, 1992) in Chinese culture. Confucian ethics reinforces the central person of guanxi in the social order, and the boundary between public and private is blurred. Therefore, the whole society is connected by guanxi circles. Guanxi is fundamentally self-centred and personal, which determines the sociocultural and political–economic dynamics in China (Wang & Rowley, 2016).

Wang and Rowley (2016) coined the three terms to illustrate how guanxi forms the socioeconomic structure in Chinese society: (1) guanxi holder: the person who stands at the centre of guanxi circles produced by his or her own social influence; (2) guanxi knot: interlinked guanxi circles influenced by the Tier 1 guanxi holder; and (3) guanxi web: a dynamic system composed of numerous guanxi knots in which all guanxi holders constantly interact and change their tiers depending on circumstances. The guanxi web is composed of numerous guanxi knots, which extends guanxi from the "Tier 1 holder" to "Tier *n* holder", and each holder can be from Tier 1 to Tier *n* in the hierarchy determined by guanxi holder's influential power.

Tsang (1998) claimed that because the Chinese represent a high-context culture, constructs of guanxi and their attributes need to be explored within their own cultural setting. The concept of business in China is not the same as in the West; instead, it is part of a holistic life of Chinese, which is intertwined with social, cultural, and political factors. To some extent, maintaining good guanxi is more important than fulfilling the contract due to the Confucian "rule of man" and holistic and long-term view of Chinese philosophy. Studying how guanxi is practised in the West, therefore, requires clarification on the distinctive characteristics exhibited by Chinese guanxi, compared to those of Western social networks (see Table 2.1 for a summary, based on past studies).

Social outlook. The concept and theory of social networks were developed with reference to individualistic societies, where the goals of individuals are valued more highly than the goals of the group (Sun & Lancaster,

Table 2.1 Characteristics distinguishing social networks and guanxi

	Social network	Guanxi
Social outlook	Individualistic (Sun & Lancaster, 2013)	Hierarchical, particularism (Chen et al., 2013)
Information capture	Weak ties have an advantage (Bian, 1997; Burt, 2000; Granovetter, 1995; Zhou, Wu, & Luo, 2007)	Reliance on strong ties (Chen et al., 2013)
Motive	Social exchange (Blau, 1964; Cropanzano & Mitchell, 2005)	Renqing (i.e. human touch and personal favour) (Chen et al., 2013; Faure & Fang, 2008)
Trust base	Cognition-based (Chua, Morris, & Ingram, 2009)	Affect base (Chen et al., 2013; Chua et al., 2009)
Nature of relation	Interdependent (Cropanzano & Mitchell, 2005; Lawler & Thye, 1999)	Dependent (Luo & Chen, 1997; Xin & Pearce, 1996)
Accessibility	Random (Moreira, Paula, Costa Filho, & Andrade, 2006)	Exclusive inner circle members (Barbalet, 2017; Chen et al., 2013; Fan, 2002)
Durability	Short- to mid-term (Hofstede, 2001)	Long-term (Lovett, Simmons, & Kali, 1999; Styles & Ambler, 2003)
Protocol	Informal (Barney, 1985)	Both informal and formal (Barbalet, 2017; Chen, Friedman, Yu, Fang, & Lu, 2009)
Guiding principle	"Rule of law"	"Rule of man" (Davies, Leung, Luk, & Wong, 1995; Fan, 2002)

2013), and actors in the network are normally in equal status. Guanxi, conversely, reflects a particularistic society (Chen et al., 2013), such as China, in which people treat different relations using different principles of social interaction; the position of actors in the guanxi circle is therefore critical due to their social status and influential power in the circle.

Information capture. In Western countries, weak-tie networks (Granovetter, 1995) and structural-hole networks (Burt, 2000) are more widely available. Weak ties are considered effective means for gaining novel information and accessing diverse pools of information sources (Zhou et al., 2007), while in guanxi circles, people seek help from strong-tie (key guanxi holders) rather than weak-tie contacts (Chen et al., 2013). Information is captured from key guanxi holders who are trustworthy.

Motive. Actors participating in social networks seek social exchange (Blau, 1964) in terms of weighing costs against benefits. Although reciprocity is the key motive for both social exchange and guanxi, in the former it can be relationships-as-transactions or relationships-as-interpersonal attachments, or both (Cropanzano & Mitchell, 2005), while in guanxi it is entwined with renqing (i.e. affection and personal favour) (Chen et al., 2013; Faure & Fang, 2008).

Trust base. Actors in social networks gain trust by demonstrating competence first, which is cognition-based trust (Chua et al., 2009); the capability to offer tangible help is crucial. In contrast, actors in the guanxi circle build trust by resonating affections first, which is affect-based trust (Chen et al., 2013; Chua et al., 2009); the emotional need is superior to rational judgement.

Nature of relation. Social networks are an informal way for people to interact based on personal will, in which actors are interdependent for mutual goals (Cropanzano & Mitchell, 2005; Lawler & Thye, 1999), while actors in a guanxi circle are dependent on guanxi holders for protection (Xin & Pearce, 1996) and making decisions (Luo & Chen, 1997) through accessing information and resources.

Accessibility. Social networks constitute a random network with a degree of distribution that unravels the size distribution of social groups (Moreira et al., 2006); they are open to anyone who wants to participate. But a guanxi circle is exclusive to the persons within a close guanxi tie (Barbalet, 2017; Chen et al., 2013); it remains as an exclusive personal asset (Fan, 2002). Hence, it requires approval of a guanxi holder for a new member to join.

Durability. Actors participating in social networks in the West normally expect reciprocity in a short- to mid-term time frame given the "short-term oriented" view (Hofstede, 2001), while actors in a guanxi circle expect long-term benefit, as it takes time to build guanxi and favour might be exchanged in the long run (Lovett et al., 1999; Styles & Ambler, 2003).

Protocol. Compared with formal organizations, the procedure for organizing social networks is informal through individual initiative among actors (Barney, 1985). For guanxi, while the organization of activities appears informal, such as through meals outside working hours and the workplace, interaction among actors needs to follow the formal hierarchy in the guanxi circle (Barbalet, 2017; Chen et al., 2009). Normally, the Tier 1 guanxi holder sets the theme and hosts the event for each specific gathering.

Guiding principle. Individual behaviour in social networks is guided by the Western "rule of law" value, for which legal codes are superior to personal relationships, while individual behaviour in a guanxi circle is guided by the Confucian "rule of man" (Davies et al., 1995; Fan, 2002), which means that the authority of the Tier 1 guanxi holder is supreme.

References

Barbalet, J. (2017). Guanxi as social exchange: Emotions, power and corruption. *Sociology*, 1–16.

Barney, J. B. (1985). Dimensions of informal social network structure: Toward a contingency theory of informal relations in organisations. *Social Networks*, *7*(1), 1–46.

Bian, Y. (1997). Bringing strong ties back in: Indirect ties, network bridges, and job searches in China. *American Sociological Review, 62*(3), 366–385.

Blau, P. M. (1964). *Exchange and power in social life*. New York, NY: Academic.

Burt, R. S. (2000). The network structure of social capital. *Research in Organisational Behavior, 22*, 345–423.

Burt, R. S., & Burzynska, K. (2017). Chinese entrepreneurs, social networks, and guanxi. *Guthrie, Management and Organisation Review, 13*(2), 221–260.

Chen, C. C., Chen, X.-P., & Huang, S. (2013). Chinese guanxi: An integrative review and new directions for future research [中国人的关系: 综合文献回顾及未来研究方向']. *Management and Organisation Review, 9*(1), 167–207.

Chen, Y., Friedman, R., Yu, E., Fang, W., & Lu, X. (2009). Supervisor-subordinate guanxi: Developing a three-dimensional model and scale. *Management and Organization Review, 5*(3), 375–399.

Child, J. (2009). Context, comparison, and methodology in Chinese management research. *Management and Organisation Review, 5*(1), 57–74.

Chua, R. Y. J., Morris, M. W., & Ingram, P. (2009). Guanxi vs networking: Distinctive configurations of affect- and cognition-based trust in the networks of Chinese vs American managers. *Journal of International Business Studies, 40*(3), 490–508.

Cropanzano, R., & Mitchell, M. S. (2005). Social exchange theory: An interdisciplinary review. *Journal of Management, 31*(6), 874–900.

Davies, H., Leung, T. K. P., Luk, S. T. K., & Wong, Y. (1995). The benefit of guanxi: The value of relationships in developing the China market. *Industrial Marketing Management, 214*(24), 207–214.

Dunfee, T. W., & Warren, D. E. (2001). Is guanxi ethical? A normative analysis of doing business in China. *Journal of Business Ethics, 32*(3), 191–204.

Dunning, J. H., & Kim, C. (2007). The cultural roots of guanxi: An exploratory study. *World Economy, 30,* 329–341.

Fan, Y. (2002). Questioning guanxi: Definition, classification and implications. *International Business Review, 11,* 543–561.

Faure, G. O., & Fang, T. (2008). Changing Chinese values: Keeping up with paradoxes. *International Business Review, 17*(2), 194–207.

Fei, X. (1992). *From the soil: The foundations of Chinese society* (G. G. Hamilton & Z. Wang, Trans.). Berkeley: University of California Press.

Granovetter, M. S. (1995). Afterword: Reconsiderations and a new agenda. In *Getting a job: A study of contacts and careers* (2nd ed., pp. 139–182). Chicago, IL: University of Chicago Press.

Hofstede, G. (2001). *Culture's consequences* (2nd ed.). London, UK: Sage.

Hung, C. F. (2004). Cultural influence on relationship cultivation strategies: Multinational companies in China. *Journal of Communication Management, 8*(3), 264–281.

Ku, H. M. (2012). *The conduct of life—The doctrine of the mean.* Forgotten Books. www.forgottenbooks.org.

Lawler, E. J., & Thye, S. R. (1999). Bringing emotions into social exchange theory. *Annual Review of Sociology, 25,* 217–244.

Lin, N. (2001). *Social capital.* Cambridge: Cambridge University Press.

Liu, P. (2016, September). A framework for understanding Chinese leadership: A cultural approach. *International Journal of Leadership in Education, 3124,* 1–13.

Lovett, S., Simmons, L. C., & Kali, R. (1999). Guanxi versus the market: Ethics and efficiency. *Journal of International Business Studies, 30,* 231–247.

Luo, Y., & Chen, M. (1997). Does guanxi influence firm performance? *Asia Pacific Journal of Management, 14,* 1–16.

Mao, Y., Peng, K. Z., & Wong, C. S. (2012). Indigenous research on Asia: In search of the emic components of guanxi. *Asia Pacific Journal of Management, 29*(4), 1143–1168.

McNally, C. A. (2011). *China's changing guanxi capitalism: Private entrepreneurs between Leninist control and relentless accumulation.* Berkeley, CA: Berkeley Electronic Press.

Moreira, A. A., Paula, D. R., Costa Filho, R. N., & Andrade, J. S. (2006). Competitive cluster growth in complex networks. *Physical Review E, 73*(6), 065101.

Nagler, J., Levina, A., & Timme, M. (2011). Impact of single links in competitive percolation. *Nature Physics, 7,* 265–270.

Styles, C., & Ambler, T. (2003). The coexistence of transaction and relational marketing: Insights from the Chinese business context. *Industrial Marketing Management, 32,* 633–642.

Sun, J., & Lancaster, S. (2013). *Chinese globalisation: A profile of people-based global connections in China.* London and New York: Routledge.

Tong, C. K. (2014). *Chinese business: Rethinking guanxi and trust in Chinese business networks.* London and New York: Springer.

Tsang, Eric W. K. (1998). Can guanxi be a source of sustained competitive advantage for doing business in China? *Academy of Management Perspectives, 12*(2).

Vanhonacker, W. R. (2004). Guanxi networks in China. *China Business Review, 3*(3), 48–53.

Wang, B. X., & Rowley, C. (2016). Business networks and the emergence of guanxi capitalism in China: The role of the 'invisible hand'. In J. Nolan, C. Rowley, & M. Warner (Eds.), *Business networks in East Asian capitalisms* (pp. 93–118). London: Elsevier.

Wang, J. (2012, July 1–10). *Collective consultation and labor's collective rights in China.* ILERA 16th World Congress.

Wellman, B., Chen, W., & Dong, W. (2001). Networking guanxi. In T. Gold, D. Guthrie, & D. Wank (Eds.), *Social networks in China: Institutions, culture, and the changing nature of guanxi* (pp. 221–241). Cambridge: Cambridge University Press.

Xin, K., & Pearce, J. L. (1996). Guanxi: Connections as substitutes for formal institutional support. *Academy of Management Journal, 39*(6), 1641–1658.

Yang, C. F. (1988). Familism and development: An examination of the role of family in contemporary China Mainland, Hong Kong, and Taiwan. In D. Sinha & H. S. R. Kao (Eds.), *Social values and development: Asian perspectives* (pp. 93–123). Delhi: Sage.

Yeung, I. Y. M., & Tung, R. L. (1996). Achieving business success in Confucian societies: The importance of guanxi (connections). *Organisational Dynamics, 25*(2), 54–65.

Zhou, H., & Long, L. (2005). A review of paternalistic leadership research. *Advances in Psychological Sciences, 13,* 227–238.

Zhou, L., Wu, W., & Luo, X. (2007). Internationalization and the performance of born-global SMEs. *Journal of International Business Studies, 38,* 673–690.

3

Guanxi Practices in Intra-firm Multicultural Groups: A Case of Chinese MNCs Operating in Europe

Abstract Many scholars have studied how guanxi plays a key role in China's cultural, social, and political environment. Guanxi is widely accepted in academia as an indigenous construct from China: deeply rooted in Chinese culture and reflected in the behaviour of Chinese people. Less is known, however, about how the employees of Chinese multi-national Companies (MNCs) employ guanxi in the West. In contrast to the common assumptions that all Chinese tend to exercise guanxi to handle social relations, this study reveals that while Chinese expatriates (CEs) actively practice guanxi with their homeland counterparts, they do not do so with host-country nationals (HCNs) and host-country Chinese (HCC). No such activities were also observed between the last two groups. The emergent model describes that guanxi practice affects intra-firm multi-cultural group dynamics in both institutional and social domains that shape the shared belief and behavioural patterns of organization members.

Keywords Chinese MNCs · Globalization · Expatriate · Guanxi · Intergroup dynamics

© The Author(s) 2019   **21**
B. X. Wang, *Guanxi in the Western Context*,
https://doi.org/10.1007/978-3-030-24001-1_3

Introduction

Chen, Chen, and Huang (2013) conducted a comprehensive review of 213 studies of Chinese guanxi and social networking at the micro- and macro-levels, crossing multiple disciplines. They concluded that guanxi tends to be a mixture of family and non-family, personal and impersonal, and social and institutional characteristics. They encapsulated guanxi research in three streams: (1) research focusing on the individual and interpersonal level, studying the domains of guanxi, the measurement of guanxi, the antecedents and outcomes of guanxi, and the factors that influence the quality of guanxi; (2) research on guanxi at an organizational level, such as firm-to-firm and firm-to-government guanxi, with a main focus on its effects on firm performance and other financial outcomes; and (3) research examining the social and moral dilemmas of guanxi, focusing mainly on how guanxi practices for the benefit of focal units may affect the superordinate units in which the subunit is embedded, as well as the tensions between traditional relational ethics as opposed to modernist professional ethics.

Chen et al. (2013) also highlighted two understudied areas: how guanxi practice affects intra-firm group dynamics and how guanxi is practised by Chinese MNCs operating outside of China. By studying how guanxi practices affect intra-firm dynamics in a Chinese MNC operating in Europe, my research addressed these two areas.

Because most research on guanxi has been conducted in China (e.g. Bian, 1997; Chen, Friedman, Yu, & Sun, 2011; Kwock, James, & Tsui, 2013; Opper, Nee, & Holm, 2017; Wong & Huang, 2015; Wong & Tam, 2000), we know little about whether and how guanxi is practised by Chinese MNCs operating outside of China (Chen et al., 2013). My research focused on guanxi practice and examined guanxi practice among different social groups in a Chinese MNC operating in Europe.

My findings revealed that guanxi was practised differently among three demographic groups: CEs, HCNs, and HCC. I observed that guanxi was practised between actors in the CE group. However, there was no guanxi practice in either the HCN group or the HCC group, or among the three groups; both the HCN and the HCC groups built their own social networks as done by other Western organizations. This study contributes theoretically to the fields of guanxi, social networks, and international business, and it sheds light on guanxi practice at the group level of intra-firm relationships in a multicultural context.

Guanxi Practice in the Chinese Context

Past research has widely studied guanxi practice in the Chinese operations of Chinese MNCs. Bian (1997) presented guanxi as bridges in job searches in China, which provided more opportunities for applicants recommended by guanxi holders associated with relevant firms. Ambler, Styles, and Xiucun (1999) found that long-term relational commitment and the need for prior guanxi in China were two successful factors for doing business. Barbalet (2017) stated that guanxi is a cultivated practice that is entered into on the basis of perceptions of opportunities for future advantage, which is particularly efficient in the situations of tight credit and high competition that prevail in small and medium enterprises. Chen, Friedman, Yu, Fang, and Lu (2009) argued that guanxi represents the infusion of family-like relations into work relations, including both the strong affective attachment and deference to hierarchy inherent in Chinese family structures. Social exchange theory implies an exchange of freedom in return for quality of work, while guanxi implies an exchange of role adherence (e.g. commitment to job, organization, and power of the supervisor) in return for being included as a family-like member in the firm.

Chen et al. (2009) also found that guanxi practice can increase employees' procedural justice perceptions. On the other hand, group-level guanxi practice, having managerial decisions systematically based on guanxi, can have a negative influence on employees' procedural justice perceptions. This indicates that those employees who are beneficiaries of guanxi practices may have an overall net-positive response to guanxi practices, while the opposite may be true for those who are not beneficiaries. It is also interesting to note that guanxi is partly utilitarian, and for those who are no longer considered profitable to know, guanxi is easily broken. Xian, Atkinson, and Meng-Lewis (2017) also found that guanxi was positively related to a high-performance work system, which is positively related to trust and job satisfaction.

Shenkar (2009) suggested that, as they internationalize, successful Chinese MNCs need to maintain the Chinese characteristics in order to implement a well-developed guanxi that can substitute for formal coordination and communication mechanisms. Research investigating whether and how guanxi is practised outside China, and with what effects, however, is still in its infancy.

Guanxi Practice in Multicultural Context

Guanxi is derived from Confucian culture and has guided the social behaviour of the Chinese for more than two millennia (Chen et al., 2013; McNally, 2011; Zhang & Zhang, 2006). These same Confucian values are likely to influence the behavioural patterns of people working in Chinese MNCs.

Research has shown that guanxi still plays a key role in internationalized Taiwanese MNCs (Chen & Easterby-Smith, 2008), as Taiwanese managers believe that trust, face (renqing), and reciprocity in personal relationships with employees are very important in managing human resources in an international organization. Guanxi practice in host countries, however, remains significantly under-investigated, and we know little about how social relationships in the branches of Chinese MNCs are guided and constrained by Chinese and Western cultural norms.

From a study of three Chinese MNCs in Denmark, Li-Ying, Stucchi, Visholm, and Jansen (2013) identified guanxi practice as one of the advantages of Chinese MNCs, because it helped firms to cultivate relationships with business partners to overcome their foreignness to the host country's institutions. Their findings show how Chinese managers relied on informal contacts and guanxi between Danish officials and the Chinese to fill a gap between a formal institutional framework, which was based on legally enforceable contracts (in Denmark), and a national culture that is accustomed to informal institutions such as guanxi and trust (in China).

Child and Marinova (2014) argued that some Chinese MNCs in the West operate in a customary way of approaching officials, which is grounded on an experience of guanxi practice in the home country; however, this customary approach may prove to be counterproductive in the host country where there is an insistence on strict adherence to formal procedure. Lin, Zhao, and Lin (2016) studied 30 CEs working in five Western countries and concluded that guanxi was helpful for expatriates, helping a candidate secure a job even if he or she did not meet the requirements but had a good relationship with the boss. Leung (2014) noted that when CEs work with local employees, difficulties may arise not from specific cultural differences but from culture-based intragroup dynamics.

My study focused on how guanxi practice affects intra-firm group dynamics in the multicultural context that characterizes the overseas operations of Chinese MNCs.

Research Method

Deng (2012) suggested that given the present state of the literature regarding the internationalization of Chinese firms, initial theory building is paramount before more elaborate theories can be tested. Rich qualitative descriptions are important to stimulate the development of these theories (Hambrick, 2007). A qualitative approach is suitable to gather rich information on topics where little is known. Because of these reasons, I conducted an exploratory case study, aiming to expand our understanding of how guanxi practice affects the multicultural group dynamics of Chinese MNCs as they expand in Europe.

Research Setting

I conducted my study in a large Chinese MNC, which I will refer to as BY to maintain confidentiality, with extensive operations in Europe. BY provides a comprehensive range of financial services to customers across the Chinese mainland. At the time of the study, outside of mainland China, BY operated in 51 countries and regions, including 18 countries in Europe. Its international operations, however, only accounted for less than 4% of both profits and assets, because its main purpose and focus were to help Chinese companies operate in overseas markets.

Many researchers (Chen et al., 2013; McNally, 2011; Tong, 2014; Zhang & Zhang, 2006) have shown that guanxi practice is strongly related to both cultural and institutional contexts. In order to ensure robustness of observation across contexts, therefore, I selected six subsidiaries in Europe, namely those located in France, Germany, Luxemburg, the Netherlands, Portugal, and the UK. These six subsidiaries represent diverse cultural clusters within Europe—Latin (France and Portugal), Anglo-Saxon (UK), and Germanic (Germany, Luxemburg, the Netherlands). They all also differ considerably from China in terms of the cultural values and institutional context that underpin guanxi. From a cultural perspective, the score of national cultural dimensions (Hofstede, 2017) between China and the six countries is significantly different in various respects (see Table 3.1), making them ideal host countries to explore the indigenous Chinese guanxi practice.

As illustrated in Table 3.1, five dimensions are directly related to the dynamic of multicultural groups and the perception of guanxi practice. In power distance, China is ranked highest, indicating that Chinese tend to accept and expect that power is distributed unequally. Given the power of the guanxi holder, Chinese expect to be treated differently according to hierarchy in the guanxi circle; however, HCNs of the rest of the six countries might find this difficult to deal with. In individualism, China is ranked lowest, indicating that Chinese tend to compromise individual needs for organizational goals as well as in the guanxi circle. Apart from Portuguese, this also might be very challenging for HCNs of the other five countries. In uncertainty avoidance, China is ranked lowest, indicating that Chinese have a low tolerance of uncertainty; Chinese employees might prefer to stay in the guanxi circle to avoid risk and to gain a sense of security. Except for the UK, HCNs of the other five countries might have a different preference. The dimension of long-term orientation is derived from Confucian culture, and here China is ranked highest, which reflects the durability of guanxi practice. Among the other six countries, Germans might feel comfortable with this. Finally, in terms of indulgence, China is ranked lowest. This is not surprising, given the Confucian meritocratic system (Warner, 2004). Chinese are willing to work hard for personal

Table 3.1 Cultural dimensions of China, France, Germany, Luxemburg, the Netherlands, Portugal, and the UK

Country	Power distance	Individualism	Masculinity	Uncertainty avoidance	Long-term orientation	Indulgence
China	80	20	66	30	87	24
France	68	71	43	86	63	48
Germany	35	67	66	65	83	40
Luxemburg	40	60	50	70	64	56
Netherlands	38	80	14	53	67	68
Portugal	63	27	31	99	28	33
UK	35	89	66	35	51	69

Source Hofstede (2001, 2017)

achievement, and actors in the guanxi circle are willing to indulge the guanxi holder rather than themselves. Among the six countries, Portuguese might have the best understanding of their diligent Chinese peers.

From an institutional perspective, the Worldwide Governance Indicators (WGI) project (Kaufmann, Kraav, & Mastruzzi, 2017) indicates substantial differences between China and the six other countries on all six dimensions of governance. Kaufmann et al. (2017) drew data on perceptions of governance from a wide variety of sources and organized them into six clusters in response to the six broad dimensions of governance. For each of these clusters, they used a statistical methodology to standardize the data from very diverse sources into comparable units and constructed an aggregate indicator of governance as a weighted average of the underlying source variable, as well constructed margins of error that reflect the unavoidable imprecision in measuring governance.

As illustrated in Table 3.2, the World Bank Group has initiated and developed the WGI project, which reports the aggregate and individual governance indicators for more than 200 countries and territories starting from 1996. The World Bank Group defined governance as "consisting of the traditions and institutions by which authority in a country is exercised. This includes the process by which governments are selected, monitored and replaced; the capacity of the government to effectively formulate and implement sound policies; and the respect of citizens and the state for the institutions that govern economic and social interactions among them" (World Bank, 2018).

It is recognizable that institutional indicators in China are far lower than those of the other six countries, and five of the six dimensions are related to the institutional context of Chinese firms. The voice and accountability dimension indicates that employees working in Chinese MNCs might not be expected to express their opinions openly and freely. Because of the low scores for government effectiveness and regulatory quality, and because most Chinese MNCs are SOEs and their management system is guided by the Chinese government, the quality of policy formulation and implementation in these firms might be far behind Western MNCs. The score for the rule of law reflects the fact that in Chinese society the "rule of man" prevails. The daily operation of Chinese MNCs, therefore, might be decided by the preferences of those wielding authority, rather than by

Table 3.2 Institutional indicators of China, France, Germany, the Netherlands, Portugal, and the UK

2016 indicator	China	France	Germany	Luxemburg	Netherlands	Portugal	UK
Voice and accountability	−1.62	1.08	1.33	1.44	1.48	1.17	1.24
Political stability and absence of violence/terrorism	−0.52	−0.06	0.76	1.41	0.89	1.02	0.83
Government effectiveness	0.36	1.41	1.74	1.69	1.84	1.22	1.61
Regulatory quality	−0.26	1.07	1.82	1.72	1.98	0.84	1.76
Rule of law	−0.22	1.41	1.61	1.71	1.89	1.13	1.63
Control of corruption	−0.25	1.37	1.83	2.08	1.95	0.96	1.88

Source Worldwide Governance Indicators (Kaufmann et al., 2017)

company policy, and personal relationships might prevail on compliance with the rules. The score for control of corruption reflects the fact that corruption is defined differently in China: a gift over the value of £50 is considered corruption in the UK, yet it is barely a presentable souvenir by Chinese standards. Gift giving at the personal level for the purpose of organizational business is indeed a controversial side of guanxi practice.

Sampling

I employed theoretical sampling (Corley & Gioia, 2004) in purposefully choosing my informants and pursuing data relevant to the themes that emerged from the ongoing analysis, and the constant comparison of data across informants. Snowball sampling was used as an appropriate approach in this study, acknowledging the importance of guanxi in the Chinese context and the challenge to locate and reach potential international participants. The chosen informants were recommended by my guanxi tie in the company (i.e. a senior manager working for BY), based on her assessment of who would be most comfortable in sharing personal views and experiences relevant to my main research question concerning how guanxi practice affects intra-firm multicultural group dynamics. Overall, the composition of my informant sample eventually reflected the demographics of BY, illustrated in Table 3.3, to be representative of what emerged as three relevant in-groups among employees: CEs, non-Chinese HCNs, and HCC. The number of employees in the table is estimated due to fluid personnel changes.

Data Collection

I collected data through semi-structured, one-on-one interviews. Chen et al. (2013) noted that the interview method was not used much in guanxi studies, and that researchers could benefit from extensive semi-structured interviews with respondents who had knowledge and experience with guanxi practices. By using semi-structured interviews, my study endeavoured to provide rich descriptions of individual experiences and, more importantly, to extend guanxi theory through new empirical insights. In

Table 3.3 Demographics of BY

Branch	No. of total employees	% of CEs	No. of informants (CEs)	% of HCCs	No. of informants (HCCs)	% of HCNs	No. of informants (HCNs)
France	200	15	2	70	6	15	2
Germany	230	17	2	70	6	13	2
Luxemburg	120	29	2	38	2	33	2
Netherlands	30	17	1	33	1	50	1
Portugal	17	29	1	41	1	30	1
UK	480	10	2	79	9	11	3
Total	1077	15	10	69	25	16	11

order to do so, a list of themes—such as "Please describe your relationship with your colleagues including Chinese expatriates, local non-Chinese, and local Chinese" and "What is your experience and how do you feel working in the group in which there are people from multicultural backgrounds?"—was generated from the literature, and open-ended questions were developed to explore and expand on these themes (Denzin & Lincoln, 2005).

I conducted a total of 46 in-depth semi-structured interviews, as detailed in Table 3.4, during the period of March 2015 to November 2017. Given the sensitive nature of the data being sought, conducting research on guanxi in a typical Chinese organization requires very good guanxi to access informants and gain their trust for collecting authentic data. It was considered best to elicit this information in the context of face-to-face, Skype, and telephone interviews to allow ample opportunity for the participants to elaborate on their response to items. The interviews lasted between 60 and 120 minutes. Most of them were tape-recorded, upon permission.

Informants varied in both the functional area and the hierarchical level that they represented. I interviewed 10 CEs who were members of a top management team in overseas subsidiaries, 25 HCC, and 11 HCN informants, ranging from the vice-president level down to the lower-middle of the hierarchy positions, such as CFO, human resource manager, local sales manager, and marketing researcher (see Table 3.4). A total of 11 interviews were conducted in English and 35 in Mandarin, depending upon the respondents' preferences. I am a native Mandarin speaker and fluent in English, so no interpreters or translations were used during the interview or the data analysis. I asked the three groups of informants similar questions, and they were constantly asked to substantiate their viewpoints with examples and elaborations. I conducted my analysis on the transcripts in their original form to avoid the risk of losing meaning through translation. I then translated illustrative quotes from Chinese into English.

In terms of the measurement of guanxi practice, scholars define guanxi strength in terms of intimacy and trust (Bian, 1997), yet they operationalize it in terms of familiarity, which is how well the guanxi parties know each other (Chen et al., 2013). Guthrie (1998) used the term guanxi practice to refer to the use of personal relations for achieving any objectives in work

Table 3.4 Informants

Branch	Informant ID	Gender	Position[a]	Year of tenure[b]	% of each group
France	CE1	F	A	30/10[c]	7% of CE
	CE2	M	B	20/6[c]	
	HCC1	M	A	28	4% of HCC
	HCC2	M	B	8	
	HCC3	F	B	3	
	HCC4	F	C	5	
	HCC5	F	C	8	
	HCC6	M	C	2	
	HCN1	M	A	6	7% of HCN
	HCN2	M	B	25	
Germany	CE3	F	A	30/10[c]	5% of CE
	CE4	F	B	18/2[c]	
	HCC7	M	B	10	4% of HCC
	HCC8	M	B	5	
	HCC9	M	C	6	
	HCC10	F	C	2	
	HCC11	F	C	10	
	HCC12	M	C	3	
	HCN3	F	B	30	7% of HCN
	HCN4	M	C	2	
Luxembourg	CE5	F	A	30/10[c]	6% of CE
	CE6	F	B	15/2[c]	
	HCC13	F	B	5	4% of HCC
	HCC14	M	C	6	
	HCN5	M	A	2	5% of HCN
	HCN6	F	C	4	
Netherlands	CE7	M	A	20/5[c]	20% of CE
	HCC15	M	C	3	10% of HCC
	HCN7	M	C	2	7% of HNC
Portugal	CE8	F	A	28/2[c]	20% of CE
	HCC16	M	C	2	14% of HCC
	HCN8	M	B	2	20% of HCN

(continued)

Table 3.4 (continued)

Branch	Informant ID	Gender	Position[a]	Year of tenure[b]	% of each group
UK	CE9	M	A	30/10[c]	4% of CE
	CE10	F	B	30/3[c]	
	HCC17	M	B	5	2% of HCC
	HCC18	M	B	8	
	HCC19	M	B	3	
	HCC20	F	B	2	
	HCC21	F	C	10	
	HCC22	M	C	3	
	HCC23	M	C	18	
	HCC24	F	C	2	
	HCC25	F	C	6	
	HCN9	M	A	10	6% of HCN
	HCN10	M	B	2	
	HCN11	F	C	10	
Total	46				

[a] A: senior management, B: middle management, C: lower-level staff
[b] As of the time of interview
[c] Years working at the branch

and life. Guanxi practices were also used as indicators of guanxi quality (Chen et al., 2013) conceived as the quality of social exchange activities outside of work between two parties (Lawler & Thye, 1999), as well as the extent to which a work relationship is transformed into a family-like, communal sharing relationship (Chen et al., 2013). Therefore, guanxi practice is here conceptualized as affective attachment, inclusion of personal life into workplace relationship and predominantly non-work-related social exchange acts, such as personal favour exchange, gift giving, and dinner invitations. As the major difference between the Chinese guanxi measurements and the Western social exchange is that the former includes social exchanges outside work whereas the latter is limited to personal relationships at work. The inclusion of non-work-related social exchange has the advantage of capturing a mixture of the affect and instrumentality of Chinese guanxi (Chen et al., 2013).

Data Analysis

I analysed these data using techniques for grounded theory building. I reviewed the data and tagged relevant excerpts from interviews with codes. As more data were collected, and re-reviewed, codes were grouped into concepts, and then into categories. These categories became the basis for theory development. Through open coding, I identified initial concepts in the data and grouped them into categories. I used sentences as coding units and labelled each textual expression with simple and descriptive phrases. I established links among codes in the next round of axial coding, wherein I searched for relationships between and among these categories, which facilitated assembling them into higher-order themes. Finally, I gathered similar themes into several overarching dimensions that make up the basis of the emergent framework. The final data structure is illustrated in Fig. 3.1, which summarizes the second-order themes on which I built the model of group dynamics affected by guanxi practice.

How Guanxi Practice Affects Intra-firm Multicultural Group Dynamics

In this section, I integrate three sets of observations, visually summarized in three displays. Figure 3.1 shows the code structure resulting from my initial analysis, Figs. 3.2 and 3.3 show the emergent theoretical framework, and Table 3.5 shows additional supporting data.

Combined, Figs. 3.2 and 3.3 highlight the core constructs in my emerging theory of how guanxi practice affects intra-firm multicultural group dynamics, as well as the different group dynamics in both the institutional domain (task-related teamwork), illustrated in Fig. 3.2, and the social domain (personal relationship) illustrated in Fig. 3.3, in the organizational context. The core constructs are displayed in Fig. 3.2: (1) group salience increased by exclusive guanxi practice; (2) out-group activation; (3) formation of superordinate group; (4) in-group prototyping. An additional construct is displayed in Fig. 3.3: (5) interplay discrepancy of demographic intergroups. This framework highlights that guanxi practice is only observed among CE members, which means that CE members con-

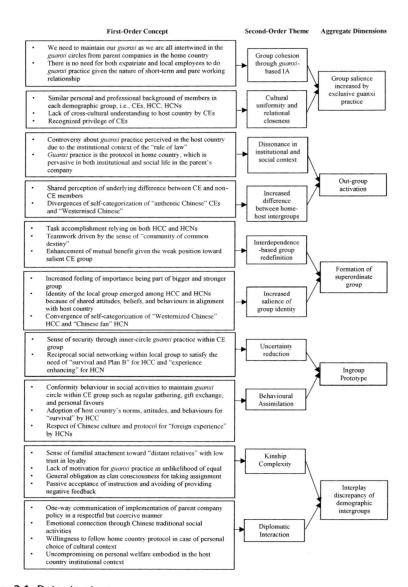

Fig. 3.1 Data structure

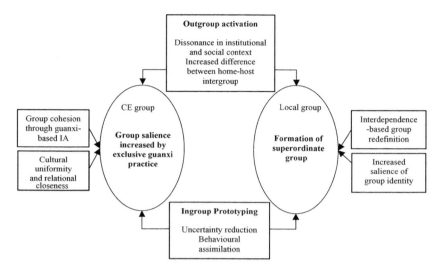

Fig. 3.2 A model of guanxi practice affecting intra-firm multicultural group dynamics in institutional domain

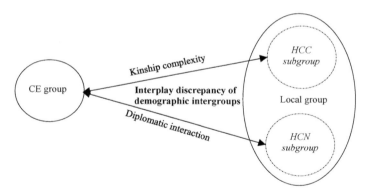

Fig. 3.3 A model of guanxi practice affecting intra-firm multicultural group dynamics in social domain

Table 3.5 Data supporting interpretation of guanxi practice affecting multicultural group dynamics

Theme	Representative quotations
	In-group salience increased by exclusive guanxi practice
Group cohesion through guanxi-based (IAs)	We need to maintain our guanxi as we got IAs through guanxi holders in headquarters in the home country, we need to help each other to ensure my IA our next step of my career path. (CE1)
	I often work at home during the holiday, we communicate by WeChat about work and personal issues, we help each other not only for work as well as personal favours. (CE3)
	It took me many years and efforts to develop guanxi in China, of course, I have benefited from it a lot. However, there is no need for me to do it with local colleagues as we won't be able to help each other for long-term career or life. (CE5)
	The way I manage staff is different, I go out with Chinese expatriate staff for dinner and their family member but not with local nationals as they don't need. (CE7)
Cultural uniformity and relational closeness	Most of us have worked for BY since we graduated from universities in China. I have worked in several departments in different parts of China. Some of us know each other before we took IAs. (CE2)
	I feel that there is huge difference between Chinese and British culture, Chinese tend to be more emotional and like to build intimate relation. Renqing plays key role in Chinese companies, we expect to be looked after by the employer and superiors. (CE9)
	Expatriates often socialize as they live in the same area, they communicate with the headquarter every day, and they chat in the office about work and personal matters. (HCC1)
	Out-group activation
Dissonance in institutional and social domains	I have lived here for 20 years, although I am Chinese, I don't like to do guanxi practice because it is not professional. Expatriates are doing this all the time. (HCC17)
	Chinese would like to have personal relationship, but British people are only communicating in relation to working but not at personal level. (CE10)
	You can achieve your own goal through good guanxi. Good guanxi is very important here for expatriates, especially with parent company, guanxi is very personal. (HCN1)

(continued)

Table 3.5 (continued)

Theme	Representative quotations
Increased difference between home-host intergroup	We mainly socialize among ourselves but not with local nationals and local Chinese, we are from similar background. Local Chinese are Chinese, but they are very different from us in terms of their values and behaviours. (CE4)
	Chinese expatriates speak Mandarin at work most of time, even in the formal meeting, I need my colleague to translate for me, however, no one would tell me what they are talking if I don't ask. (HCN3)
	Chinese expatriates have their own circle; they won't build close relationship with us. Although I am Chinese, I am not considered the same kind as expatriate as I don't have guanxi in China, probably, I am also very Westernised by their standard. (HCC7)
Formation of superordinate group	
Interdependence-based group redefinition	I don't care much about personal relationship with my colleagues, the most important thing is to do my job well, which is the key reason that I am considered valuable at BY, therefore, I really need to work closely with my local national colleagues as they know local protocol and regulations better. (HCC13)
	The local Chinese is quite different from expatriates; it is quite obvious to me. We have professional relationship and work as a team. Despite they are Chinese, I don't feel much difference between me and local Chinese. (HCN5)
Increased salience of group identity	I go out with local nationals sometimes for a drink, it is kind of network which smooth the teamwork, I quite like it. We really rely on each other to finish the task. We can be quite direct at work. (HCC18)
	I am definitely not able to join expatriate circle. I live here, therefore, I am considered local, and I feel quite comfortable about it and I have good working relationship with my other local colleagues. (HCC4)
	As expatriate, we play the key role to carry on the Chinese culture to this country, which I feel privileged, I respect local culture while I need to hold my value and culture. CEs are very important for successfully implement strategy and policy form parent company. (CE6)
	There is clear boundary between expatriates and locals, however, I think we need each other to do things. Expatriates have status privilege in this subsidiary, I am also quite lucky being local national in this country. (HCN9)

(continued)

Table 3.5 (continued)

Theme	Representative quotations
Uncertainty reduction	*Ingroup prototyping* I don't feel much cultural shock here as we have stayed in same block and lived together like a big family. (CE9) As I don't have guanxi with expatriates and parent company, I work here for survival and I really need to have good working relationship with other local colleagues. I might need their help for plan B, who know. (HCC15) I really fascinated about Chinese philosophy and culture when I studied in university, this is probably the only opportunity for me to practice what I have learnt in my home country. I don't know how long I can work here, hence, I need to work closely with other local Chinese colleagues who would help me avoid cross-cultural misunderstanding. (HCN4)
Behavioural assimilation	You can ask Chinese working 18 hours but not local nationals, they have two policies, Chinese expatriates don't mind. I do overtime regularly as I need to share some responsibilities. (HCC16) I am aware that I can't order people to do things in this country, but I have to complete the task allocated by the parent company. I try to tell the local colleagues in a nice way, hopefully, they can understand where I come from. (CE10) I studied Chinese in my university years, I know in Chinese culture that you do what you are told by the parents or teachers. I try my best not to take task as an order rather a Chinese way to implement. I do give my feedback but a bit indirect, try to be in Chinese way. (HCN2)

(continued)

Table 3.5 (continued)

Theme	Representative quotations
	Interplay discrepancy of demographic intergroups
Kinship complexity	Although they are Chinese, they have possessed local values and behaviours, I don't think they have loyalty to BY, they work here just for a job for living. On another hand, we do speak same language and share similar culture, I feel a bit easier to ask local Chinese to work overtime as they can understand better. (CE8)
	Certainly, I would benefit from guanxi if expatriates like to do it with me, however, I don't think they are interested in initiate guanxi practice with me as I won't be able to offer equal reciprocation as they expect. (HCC8)
	I understand that it is not easy for Chinese MNC operating in Europe where the business practice is so different from China. Therefore, as a Chinese, I want to contribute in my way as much as possible. Most of time, I just take tasks without asking many questions or raising concerns, I will try my best to solve it at my end. (HCC12)
Diplomatic interaction	I have 9 people in my team, including 4 Chinese expatriates who report to the General Manager directly on some so-call Chinese things. I don't feel very comfortable; I feel that I am not the real department head. Anyway, it is very Chinese, quite diplomatic. (HCN11)
	My foreign colleagues working here are very friendly and they are kind of friends to China. I understand that our way of communication at parent company might not very appropriate in this country, I have to do it, but in a very polite and respective way. We are not only expatriates but also diplomats for China. (CE6)

ducted guanxi practice exclusively among themselves but not with HCNs and HCC. Consequently, in the institutional domain (Fig. 3.2), exclusive guanxi practice activated one pair of in-/out-groups (CE and non-CE), rather than three demographic intergroups (CE, HCC, HCN). This evoked the formation of a superordinate group: a local group consisting of two subgroups (HCC and HCN). In the social domain (Fig. 3.3), three demographic intergroups are activated (CE, HCC, and HCN). Below I discuss the evidence and theoretical insights associated with each element of the model.

Group Salience Increased by Exclusive Guanxi Practice

Hogg and Terry (2000) elucidated that when a group is salient, in-group members are liked more if they embody the in-group prototype, where all members are highly prototypical with a tight network of social attraction. According to informants, the CE group was "very powerful" in host-country subsidiaries.

The exclusiveness of guanxi practice within the CE group increased the in-group salience, of which the trigger is related by two specific themes: group cohesion through guanxi-based international assignment and intra-group cultural uniformity and relational closeness.

Group cohesion through guanxi-based international assignments (IAs). Consistent with prior research (Yao, Thorn, & Doherty, 2014), guanxi was an enabling factor in the relocation and providing an international assignment opportunity for CEs. There was existing guanxi back to head office that often influenced the IAs. It was critical for CEs to maintain their guanxi with existing contacts in the home country. Individuals in each in-group of BY values harmony within a group; however, guanxi valued by the hierarchical superior CE group might be seen as a liability by other groups as they were excluded from this important activity. All CE members were interconnected in the guanxi circle developed in China, which they needed to maintain by continuing guanxi practice with guanxi holders in their home country, in order to fulfil the renqing (i.e. human touch and personal favour) and obligation. CEs were selected because of their trustworthiness, rather than their competence, by the decision-makers and guanxi holders at the parent company; trust was mainly based on good guanxi between the candidates and decision-makers. Therefore, CEs felt obliged to make extra efforts, such as working long hours during the weekend or on public holidays. As an informant explained:

> I got this job through the recommendation of my former boss, we have known each other for more than 10 years, although I moved to another department few years ago, we have kept very good guanxi. He is very helpful and influential in my career at BY. I am very grateful for this opportunity; therefore, I don't mind working overtime even during the weekend. [In this case, the former boss is the guanxi holder who helped the informant obtain an international assignment by wielding his guanxi circle.] (CE1)

Having maintained guanxi practice with guanxi holders in China, CE members had no intention of initiating guanxi practice with HCNs and HCC, due to the main reason that their contract of international assignment was from three to five years on average; guanxi practice is time-consuming and takes years to bring to fruition. Nonetheless, they needed to keep guanxi practice with each other in the host country to balance the equilibrium of the entire guanxi circle, which was led by the same guanxi holders, and it was a "community of common interest" in which all CE members were interconnected:

> We got to know each other only since we have been posted in this country, though we all worked at BY but various departments in China. It is important for us to get to know each other well [so] we can share the information from the parent company. Furthermore, one of my colleagues' current boss in China is my former boss who [was] very helpful [to] us in terms of our career path. (CE2)

Cultural uniformity and relational closeness. The CE members shared a similar background, in that most of them graduated in China with a major in a foreign language and had worked in BY ever since, expecting a lifelong career in the same organization. The homogeneous organizational culture reinforced the similar and rigid values, attitude, and behaviours in CEs towards work and life, regardless of the changes of institutional and social environments. Furthermore, the alien culture of the host country and the concentrated living environment constructed the group solidarity reinforced by the boundaryless professional and personal life, in which the organizational culture they possessed in China was intensified rather than diluted. Thus, it generated vigorous cultural uniformity:

> We live in the same building block rented by the company and often dine together, through guanxi practice, we share not only working place and business information but also the private life. We live abroad; it is crucial for us to keep the culture we have developed in China. (CE5)

Although it is recognized from above two quotes that Western expatriates located in a host country have similar experience, the CEs have strong and deep need for guanxi practice in order to create a psychological "home from home" to share or personal affections given that most CEs have lived abroad without being with close family members, i.e. spouse and children. The CE group was perceived as lacking cross-cultural understanding to exclude host-country employees from their guanxi practice, though it increased the sense of security to help CEs adapt to the host country and reduce the cultural shock. Furthermore, an IA in the developed country was a privilege and of personal benefit for Chinese managers, given the Chinese status-driven culture. The senior-level CE was perceived as the "imperial envoy", conveying messages from the parent company rather than managing daily operation of subsidiaries in the host country. The renqing-driven relational closeness based on personal favour and affection—a key connotation of guanxi—was the rationale of guanxi practice that led to greater satisfaction through improved coordination (Barnes, Yen, & Zhou, 2011):

> As Chinese people, we value very much renqing because we feel good by expressing personal feeling and exchange favours to our peers which helps me emotionally living abroad, this is also an effective way to establish harmonious working relationship. (CE7)

Consequently, exclusive guanxi practice within the CE group increased in-group salience; in the meantime, it activated the non-CE group as the out-group. Guanxi practice within the CE group was intense; however, it was a dyadic relationship involving reciprocity for both personal and work between CE members only, exclusive to other intra-firm groups (the HCC and HCN groups).

Out-Group Activation

The GLOBE study (House, Hanges, Javidan, Dorfman, & Gupta, 2004) identified China for having the highest score of in-group collectivism in comparison with six other countries, which means that among each in-group, duties and obligations are important determinants of social behaviour. There is a strong distinction between in-groups and out-groups, even if both CEs and HCC are Chinese, because they have very different backgrounds and guanxi capital. Thus, they are out-group to each other. Nevertheless, a high in-group society emphasizes relatedness with groups. Zagenczyk et al. (2015) noted that identifying ourselves with a particular cultural group places a boundary around our group (i.e. the in-group) and defines non-members as members of out-groups. The in-group and out-group distinction has proven useful in describing attitudes and behaviours both within and across cultural group boundaries (Gudykunst & Bond, 1997). Brown, Bradley, and Lang (2006), and Lauring (2011) contended that people generally view in-group members more positively than out-group members. Especially, the membership of the CE group is based on long-standing cultural and social relations. This in-group versus out-group categorization plays a significant role in Chinese intergroup interaction; therefore, guanxi defines the in-group and the out-group and states that the Chinese should be loyal and committed to those with guanxi only (Hui & Graen, 1997).

Dissonance in institutional and social domains. Due to the pervasiveness of guanxi practice in both institutional and social life in the parent company, CE members, regardless of their position in subsidiaries, played the powerful role of taking orders from the home country stakeholders, including superiors and guanxi holders, rather than simply communicating with them. Top-down management and authority obedience represented the dominant organizational culture in China, which the CE members developed and carried on in the host country. While many CE members were aware of the difference between the institutional and social protocols in the host country, their priority of strictly implementing strategy and policy of both management and business made by the home country was the key criterion to assess their performances. CEs perceived that the Chinese one-way communication with "telling" style is the effective method to interact with local colleagues:

> We are under tremendous time pressure to follow up the strategy and policy from the parent company, we receive the notice today and we are expected to make it happen tomorrow. We really don't have time to discuss with local colleagues and get their opinions. Furthermore, the parent company tend to make last-minute changes quite often, and we have to react quickly. (CE5)

Despite guanxi practice being the "daily routine" in China, CE members realized that the social practice used in China may not work in the host country; thus, they restricted guanxi practice to themselves because of the lack of motivation to initiate guanxi practice with the host-country employees, who were perceived as out-group members without links to guanxi holders in the home country.

Increased difference between home-host intergroups. There was a shared perception that underlay the difference between CE and non-CE members in terms of values, attitudes, and behaviour. The one-way communication style is a typical cultural trait in Chinese MNCs, although it was perceived by HCNs and HCC as against the Western values of information sharing, open discussion, and mutual respect. In addition, CEs initiated no guanxi practice towards HCNs and HCC, as they believed that HCNs, unlike Chinese, prefer a simple manager–subordinate relationship with the need for a clear direction of specific task rather than a relationship on a personal level. This provoked the divergent self-categorizations of "authentic Chinese" CEs and "Westernised Chinese":

> Although we share a similar national culture with local Chinese, they are local residents and quite Westernised, they prefer the Western management

style which is detached professional and task-driven, moreover, they do not understand Chinese organisational culture. I only have few years' assignment and I really don't have time and motivation to building close relationship with local employees including Chinese and non-Chinese. (CE7)

Most of the CEs felt that it was easier to manage HCN and HCC subordinates in the host country than to manage Chinese subordinates in the home country, as there they did not need to spend time on guanxi practice. CE members believed that HCC worked at BY for an interim arrangement without loyalty, as they preferred to work for local companies:

I can see that the local Chinese employees have no loyalty to BY as they are constantly looking for opportunity of working in local firm in order to integrate into local society for the recognition and privileged status in developed country. I don't think it is necessary to do guanxi practice with them. (CE3)

However, CEs' assumption about HCNs might be a "toxic assumption" according to HCC informants:

Chinese expatriates have their own guanxi circle and they have no intention to involve us although I am Chinese, I kind of understand that they don't think we can reciprocate in the way they are doing in China and they don't trust us very much. I feel like second class citizen, the way they treat us is as same as they treat local nationals, which is quite professional but detached, the local nationals are fine as it is their culture. However, I am Chinese, of course, I prefer more renqing at work. Anyway, I don't have much expectation. (HCC2)

Building trust in groups is the key success factor to achieve a high-performance group, in terms of cognition-based trust and affect-based trust (Chen, Eberly, Chiang, Farh, & Cheng, 2014). Groups may be able to attain the affect-based trust more quickly through guanxi practice.

CEs perceived HCNs as taking the opportunity to have a "Chinese experience" but not for a long-term commitment. Moreover, guanxi practice was alien to non-Chinese who grew up in the "rule of law" society:

Local nationals are "foreigners" and they will never understand Chinese culture and guanxi practice; in particular, they are too rational to appreciate human touch and personal favour. We value renqing very much and would like to do extra work for helping colleagues and BY; however, they are self-benefit driven. (CE8)

Therefore, the exclusive guanxi practice built a clear boundary between the CE group and other intergroups, which activated the superordinate group: a local group consisting of two subgroups (i.e. HCC and HCNs).

Formation of Superordinate Group

Hogg and Terry (2000) noted that the nature of relations between subgroups is a function of the nature of the subgroups' relationship to the superordinate group. They argued that subgroups often resist attempts by a superordinate group to dissolve subgroup boundaries and merge them into one large group, which tends to be very large, amorphous, and impersonal. People strive for a balance between conflicting motives for inclusion or sameness (i.e. satisfied by group membership) and for distinctiveness or uniqueness. However, according to their experiments, Hornsey and Hogg (1999) found that inter-subgroup relations were more harmonious when the subgroups were salient within the context of a salient superordinate group than when the superordinate group or the subgroups alone were salient. The local group emerged from the spontaneous merger of HCN and HCC subgroups, which was triggered by the immense salience of the CE group.

Interdependence-based group redefinition. Given its increased salience, the CE group created strong interdependence between HCC and HCN groups as to which they need to accomplish tasks to demonstrate their competence, which is the key criterion for measuring their performance. Therefore, both HCC and HCNs needed to redefine their group from culture-based to task-driven working groups in the sense of a "community of common destiny". Consequently, the formation of an interdependence-based local group enhanced the mutual benefit of both HCC and HCN groups, given their weak position towards the CE group.

The HCN group was very diversified and multicultural, consisting of various nationalities and races, including white European, Latin, and Asian. The common motive for the non-Chinese local nationals working for BY whom I interviewed was the personal interest in either Chinese or Asian culture. A few informants had worked for Japanese companies before they joined BY. In general, HCNs considered BY as a Chinese company rather than a global company, because of its highly centralized structure and strong national culture. There were a few HCNs working at a managerial level because of their expertise for the local market, and most of them worked for BY either for the job itself or for survival. HCNs maintained business relationships with external parties such as local authorities and clients. They believed that CEs had a closer relationship with Chinese employees because they spoke and communicated in Mandarin at work and had lunch together. The HCNs believed that there was no need for guanxi, as they were local, without guanxi holders in the parent company. They observed guanxi practice among CEs and believed it to be useful in a Chinese company; however, they felt uncomfortable about CEs communicating in Mandarin all the time:

> Chinese is the main working language in this branch. I really have to rely on my local Chinese colleagues to translate for me, such as documents or e-mails from China, as well as in some meetings. I feel quite annoyed about this, although I understand it is the way to get things done easily, but only to Chinese. (HCN6)

CEs used WeChat, a Chinese software application, to share work-related topics at any time during the day, as the Chinese believed this to be the most efficient way to sort things out, enhance personal relationships, and build a network. HCNs felt quite uncomfortable in being contacted for work-related issues after work:

> I don't use WeChat, although my Chinese boss has tried to persuade me. I don't like to be reached at any time, particularly at home, as I want to keep clear boundary between work and life. Furthermore, WeChat becomes the official channel for CEs to share some information and circulate some official documents but mainly in Chinese. They also share personal stuff, I guess it

is the way to build close relationship. However, I still prefer to use company e-mail for professional matters. (HCN7)

The HCC group was recruited locally in host countries. Some of them were born in the host country, and some have stayed since they finished their study there. Some HCC expressed their experience of "reverse cultural shock", as they felt more comfortable working with HCNs than with CEs. This was mainly due to the exclusiveness of guanxi practice within the CE group. Despite speaking Mandarin, HCC did not have any guanxi in relation to the parent company in China. They observed the intense guanxi practice among CEs, yet they were not invited to participate. Informants believed that they had earned the respect and trust from CEs through their hard work; this trust, however, was based on cognition, not affect:

> I have worked here for six years, mainly for "survival," as it is not easy for a Chinese [person] to get a job in [a] non-Chinese company outside China. I appreciate that guanxi practice is crucial in China for building a successful career; however, I don't have a chance to do so in BY because I don't have any guanxi in BY China. Thus, I am not in the guanxi circle of CEs. My value for BY is my technical competence of local market to accomplish the task allocated by the parent company, which CEs have to rely on local nationals; therefore, I need to work closely with my local non-Chinese colleagues as they understand the local protocol and regulations. Furthermore, because I speak Mandarin, it is easier for CEs to communicate. I also don't mind working overtime sometimes given my Chinese values that we take work as priority than our personal life. (HCC9)

Increased salience of group identity. Thomas (2012) argued that for Chinese, the establishment of a common group identity among non-Chinese members might be more difficult than the guanxi practice among Chinese members. However, under the circumstances, group members' willingness to participate depended on the salience of the task group identity versus that of their cultural group. In the six subsidiaries, despite the HCC group having four times the number of members (744) than CEs (163) or HCNs (170), the group salience was much less due to their low influence, without guanxi, in the organization. Even though the HCN group was in a better position to access local resources, as the "first class citizen" in the host country, they were more like local staff working for the Chinese Embassy who were expected to follow decisions rather than jointly making decisions. Hence, both HCC and HCN groups felt part of a bigger and stronger local group.

The identity of the local group was formed by sharing a similar attitude, belief, and behaviour in conformity with the institutional context of the host country:

> Although I am Chinese from mainland China where renqing and guanxi is valued most in any context, I have learned here that I need to be more Western-like to add value to BY, CEs trust me because of my competence of working with local stakeholders. I will never able to access the inner-circle of top management without guanxi in China. Therefore, I have behaved like a "Westerner" and worked with my local colleagues more closely. (HCC3)

In-group Prototyping

The perceptual accentuation of intragroup similarities and intergroup differences maximized separateness and clarity (Hogg & Terry, 2000). According to the context of BY subsidiaries in the host country, as both the CE group and the local group became salient, the members of both groups came to see themselves less as individuals and more as interchangeable exemplars of the group prototype, which is not an objective reality but rather a subjective sense of the defining attributes of a social category (Hornsey, 2008). Self-categorization was a key psychological process in group behaviour, whereby, through a process of "depersonalization", individuality was temporarily submerged within conformity to a group prototype containing idealized characteristics of the group (Liu, Li, & Yue, 2010).

Uncertainty reduction. In order to reduce subjective uncertainty about one's perceptions, attitudes, feelings, behaviours, self-concept, and place within the social world (Hornsey, 2008), all members within both the CE and local groups depersonalized themselves to generate social identity. Thus, they categorized themselves into an in-group and an out-group to accentuate the perceived similarity of the in-group prototype (Hogg & Terry, 2000). In doing so, CE members conducted intense guanxi practice within their group to preserve their strong social identity of "authentic Chinese":

> [Although] BY is the first globalized Chinese MNC, fundamentally, we are a Chinese company and we ought to possess strong Chinese characteristics in our daily operations wherever we go. Maintaining good and close guanxi with colleagues in China, as well as expatriates, is essential for us to keep our Chinese identity, which I am proud of and makes me feel secure. (CE8)

Consequently, HCC and HCN members established reciprocal social networking within the local group for an individual need of "survival and Plan B" for the HCC and "experience enhancing" for the HCNs:

> I feel more comfortable to work with HCC than CEs as they are quite straight forward and simple, and we can communicate easily and understand each other clearly. We rely on each other to complete the task. Occasionally, we go out for a drink just for fun. The local Chinese are quite different from Chinese expatriates: they are more friendly and easy going. We have good teamwork. I quite enjoy working at BY, which provides me a good opportunity to practice what I learned about Chinese culture and philosophy. (HCN8)

Behavioural assimilation. To the extent that access to the dominant group does not present too much difficulty, individual assimilation may occur (Tajfel, 1982). I observed behavioural assimilation in both the CE and local groups. Liu and Lee (2008) argued that having worked for the company in its home location, the expatriate was likely to adapt to the corporate culture through assimilation and socialization. Despite CE members having no intention of initiating guanxi practice with out-group members (i.e. the local group), some of them expected local colleagues to get things done through guanxi practice with the host-country business partners:

> My superior is a Chinese expatriate, and she asked me to get the best deal from local suppliers under the circumstance that we may not sign the contract in time, as it took a long time to process and get official approval from the parent company in China. I said it is unlikely. Then, she expected me to

use my guanxi to sort it out. But we don't do guanxi practice in this country. (HCN5)

It took a while for some CE members to realize that they needed to adapt to the local institutional and social environment in terms of their management and communication styles. According to informants, they intended to adopt a Western management style to work with local members, and guanxi practice was not appreciated in the West:

> I tried to establish guanxi with local nationals, but I failed miserably. I realized that Westerners lack human touch, and they won't help you when you need them as a friend. Their personal welfare and legal regulations are much more important than personal relationship and friendship, which I found very hard to accept. Hence, I just keep professional working relationship with local colleagues and partners and I won't build a personal or intimate relationship with them. (CE9)

Within the local group, members of the HCC subgroup went through "dual" assimilation. As local-based Chinese, they strived to adopt local values and behaviours to integrate into the culture and society of the host country. On the other hand, they also made efforts to be accepted and valued by CE members. Being "Westernised Chinese", they were perceived as lacking "authenticity" to both Chinese and Western cultures; nevertheless, they were the "bridge" across cultures:

> I have lived in this country for almost 20 years, I am quite used to the local culture and protocols, although it took me a few years to adapt. I tried to get a job in local companies, but it was extremely difficult as a Chinese. I am glad that I had a chance to work for BY. I was aware that I was recruited because I am Chinese, and I am expected to behave like Chinese towards Chinese boss. However, I felt a bit of reversed "cultural shock" at the beginning, in terms of the Chinese expatriates' working styles. I was a bit annoyed with their exclusive guanxi practice among themselves; however, after a while, I did not mind as I don't like guanxi practice anyway, and I feel better when I work with my local colleagues, regardless if they are Chinese or non-Chinese. (HCC25)

In addition, despite the fact that noticeable individual assimilation of HCN members was not expected, most informants proclaimed their adaptation working for BY:

> I like and studied Chinese culture and philosophy, I expected to practice what I learned about China by working for BY. I tried to communicate with my Chinese colleagues in a Chinese way, which is very hierarchical culture. I call my boss President Wang as the same way of all other Chinese address him. I can observe clearly the guanxi practice among Chinese expatriates. Obviously, they have a special relationship. My deputy is Chinese expatriate, he always goes to President Wang directly without involving me. I am a bit annoyed, but I understand this is Chinese culture, guanxi is essential in Chinese MNCs. (HCN2)

HCNs did not understand why HCC never disagreed with their boss, even if their boss was wrong. The value of the power distance index of the other four countries is lower than that of China. Also, they did not perceive the inequality between themselves and their boss. One informant shared his experience that one HCN subordinate challenged him over an unrealistic request of working overtime to translate a document from Chinese to English and then to Portuguese. This HCN showed him the evidence to prove that the internal employees were not able to do a proper job by sacrificing their personal time. The evidence convinced the informant and, as a result, the informant outsourced the job to an external party. The courage that the HCN possessed to confront his superior was from his belief in his judgement and his confidence in the mutual trust and benefit between him and the informant. In fact, it took the HCN one and a half years to gain the trust from the informant by building a good personal relationship and prove his competence at work. Hence, proper building of guanxi may help people from different cultures understand each other and reduce the perception of inequity between hierarchies.

Interplay Discrepancy of Demographic Intergroups

The influence of guanxi practice on group dynamics was analysed in the previous discussion from an institutional perspective of the organizational context in BY host-country subsidiaries, in which one pair of in-/out-groups (i.e. the CE and local groups) was studied. As illustrated in Fig. 3.2, the group dynamic from the social perspective, indicated in dotted lines, reveals two pairs of in-/out-groups (i.e. CE/HCC and CE/HCN) between which there is discrepancy in terms of intergroup interplay.

Kinship complexity. In this context, it was fictive kinship to distinguish the interplay between CE and HCC and between CE and HCN, given that guanxi was derived from kinship and the kinship guanxi base is more important (Tong, 2014) for Chinese. The interplay between CE and HCC was observed as the familial attachment towards "distant relatives". The complex feeling was mutual between CE and HCC members, although they were all originally from mainland China and shared the same value: that renqing is important for any relationship in both an institutional and social context.

In China, guanxi is the golden thread that ties the entire society together; therefore, everyone working for the same organization weaves the guanxi web, in which all guanxi holders are interconnected in one way or another. However, it seems that the Chinese guanxi web could not easily stretch beyond national borders, which may create a challenge in the process of the globalization of Chinese MNCs. Specifically, one of the trade-offs for Chinese living abroad was to loosen the connection with the guanxi web in China. HCC members working for BY were recruited in the host country, and they did not have guanxi holders in the parent company; however, they were in a tricky position, because they were not trusted as the close family member, yet they were expected to behave like a family member, even though they were "long distance relatives". Therefore, CE members had a sense of familial responsibility towards HCC, and they also wished or expected HCC to fulfil the duty of "family members" like in a parent's company, such as taking orders from the top, doing what they were told, and coming to work at any time they were needed:

I understand that the way I interact with local Chinese should be different from that in the home country, though they are also Chinese. We have a different background, as I am assigned by the parent's company having both privilege and obligation, but we also care and look after local Chinese in many ways. Compared to Western companies, we value renqing or human touch. Hence, local Chinese are Chinese after all and they should appreciate what BY offered for them and make a contribution to the family when needed. (CE5)

For HCC members, they had a sense of "obligation" towards BY not only because BY provided the job but also because of the emotional attachment of the "family members from home". However, they were in between two cultures; specifically, they were making a choice between working overtime for the organization (i.e. big family) and personal arrangements with family or friends (i.e. small family):

I know that almost everybody in China work overtime and leaves family behind; organisational life is more important than personal life. I live in this country and possess the local attitude of work-life balance; however, I was asked periodically to work during weekends or on public holidays. As a Chinese, I tried to comply and compromise my personal life as much as I can, but sometimes I said "No" because I want to keep my own life as normal as local nationals. Chinese expatriates don't mind sacrificing their personal life as they have status and privilege as a compensation, but I don't. (HCC24)

Diplomatic interaction. Notwithstanding that the working relationship between CEs and HCNs was normal and professional, the disparate ideological background of CEs was developed in China, whereby a holistic but solitary system intertwines with politics, the social culture, and the economy. Consequently, they were mindful of Western culture and values, either psychologically or even unconsciously. Unlike Western expatriates, CEs needed to be the "ambassadors" in addition to businesspeople; thus, "politically correct" was rather cardinal determining their career path, and they needed to become a politically astute "diplomat" prior to being a savvy businessperson. Working in the "embassy" was challenging for both CEs and HCNs, despite HCNs perceiving the challenge as a cultural difference rather than an ideological disparity. CEs' attitude towards HCNs can be described as "polite but cohesive", especially given the pressure from the home country. CEs used one-way communication to get things done in the host country, which the HCNs found difficult to take:

Working in the host country, I need to be aware that I am representing not only BY but also China. I respect local culture and values, but I need to hold onto my own culture and beliefs developed in China. I have good working relations with my foreign colleagues (i.e., HCNs); however, sometimes, I have to tell them to implement the policy from the parent company as we have no other choice but to follow. I am aware that I was quite direct, but I am always direct in a polite way. (CE9)

I understand that obeying authority is one of the key features of Chinese culture, but I still think that Chinese expatriates need to understand that they can't get things done in the same way they do in China. I try not to say "No" when I was asked to follow up something, as I appreciate "face" is important for Chinese, but I have said "No" if I believe it couldn't be done or I was not able to accept. They were not happy, and they usually try to persuade me. If I insisted, they would find someone else to accept. However, they are quite polite and respectful. I want to know them better and involve into their guanxi circle, but I realized after a while that I will never able to be involved as a "foreigner." (HCN3)

China is a family-centric country deeply rooted in Confucian ethics, which favours relationships with others (Luo & Chen, 1997), where national interests are above everything else and family interests are higher than personal interests; therefore, business interests are higher than those of employees. Chinese enterprises expect employees to regard enterprises as their family, which means that employees are expected to sacrifice personal interests when needed. Chinese employees do not view working overtime as a personal sacrifice and are even proud of it. In many Western countries, however, an individual's family comes first, and overtime not only reflects low efficiency but also signifies employees' sacrifice of personal interests and disrespect for their families. If Chinese MNCs put forward the same requirement on employees of host countries, the conflict may be self-evident.

Discussion and Conclusion

Hogg and Terry (2000) studied social identity and group dynamics in organizational contexts and stated that social attraction is produced by prototype-based depersonalization of in-group members, and personal attraction is generated by feelings that are the idiosyncrasies and complementarities of close and enduring interpersonal relationships. They also argued that social attraction may foster organizational cohesion, but interpersonal attraction may fragment the organization. However, this study shows that guanxi practice, a "daily routine" across institutional and social boundaries in the home country, is intensively performed among CE members who are both highly prototypical and relational to maintain in-group salience. Therefore, guanxi practice is a pattern of social dynamics containing both social and personal attraction, which can foster either cohesion or deviance of the group, depending on the institutional and social context.

My study reveals that guanxi practice fosters the cohesion of the CE group and merges the HCC and HCN groups, but it enlarges the social distance between two Chinese groups: the CE group and the HCC group. Consequently, exclusive guanxi practice within the CE group fosters organizational cohesion in the host country. Therefore, making the subgroup and superordinate group identity simultaneously salient is a sound strategy for managing inter-subgroup relations within a larger group. In particular, conflict arising from sociodemographic diversity within a multicultural organization can be moderated by crosscutting demography with role assignments or by encouraging a strategy of cultural pluralism (Hogg & Terry, 2000). Their proposition, although literally true, is nevertheless a consequence of "survival instinct" rather than strategy implementation, as revealed in this study.

Findings from 46 interviews provide new insights on how guanxi is practised in the international operations of Chinese MNCs. Over the past five decades, in the field of management, cultural transferability has been mainly studied as occurring from the West to the East. The time is ripe, however, to begin considering cultural transferability in both directions. This research indicates that Chinese managers have not conducted guanxi practice effectively in the host country in foreign locations. They are not aware that the guanxi practice skill cannot be transferred directly to cross-cultural contexts.

Paradox of Guanxi Practice

This study extends Liu et al.'s (2010) research, combining social identity theory with an indigenous Chinese psychology based on a sociology of social roles. It is also consistent with their finding that guanxi clearly deals with instrumental relationships. Nevertheless, the paradox I observed is that guanxi practice helped CEs a great deal for the IA adjustment. However, its strict exclusiveness within the CE group disengaged another ethnic group (HCC) while facilitating the formation of a superordinate group (the local group), which was merged by two intergroups (HCC and HCN groups). Consequently, guanxi practice triggered intra-firm multicultural group dynamics in both institutional and social forms, whereby the institutional form occurred in interplay in the CE/local group. This means that in the instrumental context of completing "rational" tasks, the HCC group perceives its identity as the same as that of HCNs—competence-based employees—and the CE group expects the same from both the HCC and HCN groups; while a social form occurred in interplay between the CE/HCC and CE/HCN groups, in the expressive context of communicating emotions, the HCC group has a strong Chinese identity of "second class citizen", and the CE group expects the HCC group to better understand the "Chinese way". On the other hand, being Chinese, the unspoken psychological contract held by HCC was that they wanted to be trusted at both the cognition base and the affect base; however, CEs focused only on the former one due to either deliberately reducing emotional dependence or being unaware of HCC's needs.

Boundarylessness of Professional and Private Domain

Apart from e-mail, WeChat[1] is the most popular Chinese social media platform via smartphone, and it is the best and official communication channel at BY. The CEs and HCC feel fairly comfortable in being reached by WeChat and share work-related topics at any time of the day, as long as the smartphone is in use. Chinese believe this is the most efficient way to sort things out and build guanxi to form in-group trust. HCNs feel quite uncomfortable in being reached for work-related issues after work. In particular, work–life balance and family responsibility are the key values in the West. Under these circumstances, Chinese MNCs need to identify the key cultural factors to escalate their globalization in the developed markets.

Practical Implications

The implications of these findings are apparent at different levels. First, there is a need to recognize the influence of guanxi practice in multicultural groups. Operating in the host country does not necessarily indicate that local nationals are insensible to the social culture of the home country, such as guanxi practice. On the contrary, it can affect both institutional and social domains in intra-firm multicultural groups. Considering the guanxi practice as an opportunity for improving group cohesion in the multicultural context, it is also a sound strategy for managing global teams of MNCs.

Second, the key insights involve the recognition for CEs, who might be more effective in achieving institutional goals through guanxi practice or an adapted version of guanxi practice to increase the engagement level of HCC and HCNs. Their achievement of an IA for the organization is crucial, and there is a need for the organization to institutionalize their

---

[1]WeChat (Chinese: 微信; pinyin: *Wēixìn*; literally: "micro-message") is a Chinese multi-purpose messaging, social media, and mobile payment app developed by Tencent. It is one of the world's largest standalone mobile apps by monthly active users with over 1 billion monthly active users. It is also known as China's "app for everything" and a "super app" because of its wide range of functions and platforms (Wikipedia).

knowledge (Inkson & King, 2012) and reap the benefits of their experiences while they are in the host country (Yao et al., 2014).

Finally, my research suggests that, in a business environment outside China, the more skilled an individual is at guanxi practice, the more likely that this expatriate will find it difficult to socialize with local nationals. Thus, when cultivating working relationships in the West, an expatriate may want to adjust his or her way of guanxi practice with local nationals, and it may not be sufficient to either cease or imitate guanxi practice in local groups.

Limitations

The study has several limitations due to its exploratory nature. While the sample is within one organization, it is selected to be representative and provide rich data and insight to develop a deeper understanding of the intra-firm guanxi practice of Chinese MNCs operating in the West. Future studies could investigate more organizations with different backgrounds, such as Chinese private companies operating in the West. Moreover, it would be worth exploring research on international HR management of Chinese MNCs that blend guanxi and social network ties into a specific organizational culture.

References

Ambler, T., Styles, C., & Xiucun, W. (1999). The effect of channel relationships and guanxi on the performance of inter-province export ventures in the People's Republic of China. *International Journal of Research in Marketing, 16,* 75–87.

Barbalet, J. (2017). Guanxi as social exchange: Emotions, power and corruption. *Sociology,* 1–16.

Barnes, B. R., Yen, D., & Zhou, L. (2011). Investigating guanxi dimensions and relationship outcomes: Insights from Sino-Anglo business relationships. *Industrial Marketing Management, 40*(4), 510–521.

Bian, Y. (1997). Bringing strong ties back in: Indirect ties, network bridges, and job searches in China. *American Sociological Review, 62*(3), 366–385.

Brown, L. M., Bradley, M. M., & Lang, P. J. (2006). Affective reactions to pictures of ingroup and outgroup members. *Biological Psychology, 71*(3), 303–311.

Chen, C. C., Chen, X.-P., & Huang, S. (2013). Chinese guanxi: An integrative review and new directions for future research [中国人的关系: 综合文献回顾及未来研究方向']. *Management and Organisation Review, 9*(1), 167–207.

Chen, I. C. L., & Easterby-Smith, M. (2008). Is guanxi still working, while Chinese MNCs go global? The case of Taiwanese MNCs in the UK. *Human Systems Management, 27*(2), 131–142.

Chen, X.-P., Eberly, M. B., Chiang, T. J., Farh, J. L., & Cheng, B. S. (2014). Affective trust in Chinese leaders: Linking paternalistic leadership to employee performance. *Journal of Management, 40*(3), 796–819.

Chen, Y., Friedman, R., Yu, E., Fang, W., & Lu, X. (2009). Supervisor-subordinate guanxi: Developing a three-dimensional model and scale. *Management and Organization Review, 5*(3), 375–399.

Chen, Y., Friedman, R., Yu, E., & Sun, F. (2011). Examining the positive and negative effects of guanxi practices: A multi-level analysis of guanxi practices and procedural justice perceptions. *Asia Pacific Journal of Management, 28*(4), 715–735.

Child, J., & Marinova, S. (2014). The role of contextual combinations in the globalisation of Chinese firms. *Management and Organisation Review, 10*(3), 347–371.

Corley, K. G., & Gioia, D. A. (2004). Identity ambiguity and change in the wake of a corporate spin-off. *Administrative Science Quarterly, 49*(2), 173–208.

Deng, P. (2012). The internationalization of Chinese firms: A critical review and future research. *International Journal of Management Reviews, 14*, 408–427.

Denzin, N., & Lincoln, Y. (2005). *The Sage handbook of qualitative research* (3rd ed.). Thousand Oaks, NJ: Sage.

Gudykunst, W. B., & Bond, M. H. (1997). Intergroup relations across cultures. In J. Berry, M. Segall, & Ç. Kağltçlbaşl (Eds.), *Handbook of cross-cultural psychology* (Vol. 3, pp. 119–161). Needham Heights, MA: Allyn & Bacon.

Guthrie, D. (1998). The declining significance of guanxi in China's economic transition. *The China Quarterly, 154*, 254–282.

Hambrick, D. C. (2007). The field of management's devotion to theory: Too much of a good thing? *Academy of Management Journal, 50*, 1346–1352.

Hofstede, G. (2001). *Culture's consequences* (2nd ed.). London, UK: Sage.

Hofstede, G. (2017). www.geert-hofstede.com/luxemburg.html.

Hogg, M. A., & Terry, D. J. (2000). Social identity and self-categorization processes in organisational contexts. *The Academy of Management Review, 25*(1), 121.

Hornsey, M. J. (2008). Social identity theory and self-categorization theory: A historical review. *Social and Personality Psychology Compass, 2*(1), 204–222.

Hornsey, M. J., & Hogg, M. A. (1999). Subgroup differentiation as a response to an overly-inclusive group: A test of optimal distinctiveness theory. *European Journal of Social Psychology, 29,* 543–550.

House, R. J., Hanges, P. J., Javidan, M., Dorfman, P. W., & Gupta, V. (2004). *Culture, leadership, and organisations: The GLOBE study of 62 societies.* Thousand Oaks, CA: Sage.

Hui, C., & Graen, G. (1997). Guanxi and professional leadership in contemporary Sino-American joint ventures in mainland China. *The Leadership Quarterly, 8*(4), 451–465.

Inkson, K., & King, Z. (2012). Contested terrain in careers: A psychological contract model. *Human Relations, 64*(1), 37–57.

Kaufmann, D., Kraav, A., & Mastruzzi, M. (2017). *The worldwide governance indicators.* Retrieved from http://info.worldbank.org/governance/wgi/#home.

Kwock, B., James, M., & Tsui, A. (2013). Doing business in China: What is the use of having a contract? The rule of law and guanxi when doing business in China. *Journals of Business Studies Quarterly, 4*(4), 56–68.

Lauring, J. (2011). Intercultural organisational communication: The social organizing of interaction in international encounters. *Journal of Business Communication, 48*(3), 231–255.

Lawler, E. J., & Thye, S. R. (1999). Bringing emotions into social exchange theory. *Annual Review of Sociology, 25,* 217–244.

Leung, K. (2014). Globalisation of Chinese firms: What happens to culture? *Management and Organisation Review, 10*(3), 391–397.

Lin, Z., Zhao, Z., & Lin, Z. (2016). Culture, expatriation and performance: Case of Chinese multinational enterprises. *Chinese Management Studies, 10*(2), 346–364.

Liu, C.-H., & Lee, H.-W. (2008). A proposed model of expatriates in multinational corporations. *Cross Cultural Management, 15*(2), 176–193.

Liu, J. H., Li, M. C., & Yue, X. D. (2010). Chinese social identity and intergroup relations: The influence of benevolent authority. In M. H. Bond (Ed.), *The oxford handbook of Chinese psychology.* Oxford University Press.

Li-Ying, J., Stucchi, T., Visholm, A., & Jansen, J. S. (2013). Chinese multinationals in Denmark: Testing the eclectic framework and internalization theory. *Multinational Business Review, 21*(1), 65–86.

Luo, Y., & Chen, M. (1997). Does guanxi influence firm performance? *Asia Pacific Journal of Management, 14*, 1–16.

McNally, C. A. (2011). *China's changing guanxi capitalism: Private entrepreneurs between Leninist control and relentless accumulation.* Berkeley, CA: Berkeley Electronic Press.

Opper, S., Nee, V., & Holm, H. (2017). Risk aversion and guanxi activities: A behavioral analysis of CEOs in China. *Academy of Management Journal, 60*(4), 1504–1530.

Shenkar, O. (2009). Becoming multinational: Challenges for Chinese firms. *Journal of Chinese Economic and Foreign Trade Studies, 2*(3), 149–162.

Tajfel, H. (1982). Social psychology of intergroup relations. *Annual Review of Sociology, 33,* 1–39.

Thomas, D. C., & Liao, Y. (2012, October 1–20). Inter-cultural interactions: The Chinese context. In *Oxford handbook of Chinese psychology.* Oxford: Oxford University Press.

Tong, C. K. (2014). Rethinking guanxi and trust in Chinese business networks. In *Chinese business.* London and New York: Springer.

Warner, M. (2004). *Management in China: Past, present and future.* London: Routledge.

WeChat's world. (2016, August 6). *The Economist.*

WeChat now has over 1 billion active monthly users worldwide. (2018, March 5). *TechNode.*

Wikipedia. https://en.wikipedia.org/wiki/WeChat#cite_note-14.

Wong, M., & Huang, P. (2015, July). Culturally embedded mechanism, guanxi in marketing. *Open Journal of Open Science, 3*, 154–158.

Wong, Y. H., & Tam, J. L. M. (2000). Mapping relationships in China: Guanxi dynamic approach. *Journal of Business & Industrial Marketing, 15*(1), 57–70.

World Bank. (2018). http://info.worldbank.org/governance/wgi/index.aspx#home.

Xian, H., Atkinson, C., & Meng-Lewis, Y. (2017, May). Guanxi and high performance work systems in China: Evidence from a state-owned enterprise. *The International Journal of Human Resource Management, 5192,* 1–20.

Yao, C., Thorn, K., & Doherty, N. (2014). Boundarylessness as a dynamic construct: The case of Chinese early career expatriates. *Career Development International, 19*(6), 683–699.

Zagenczyk, T. J., Cruz, K. S., Cheung, J. H., Scott, K. L., Kiewitz, C., & Galloway, B. (2015). The moderating effect of power distance on employee responses to psychological contract breach. *European Journal of Work and Organisational Psychology, 24*(6), 853–865.

Zhang, Y., & Zhang, Z. (2006). Guanxi and organizational dynamics in China: A link between individual and organizational levels. *Journal of Business Ethics, 67*(4), 375–392.

4

Developing Guanxi in the West: Chinese Expatriates' Adjustment in Europe

Abstract As China's global presence continues to grow, Chinese expatriates have increasingly taken up international assignments (IAs) around the world. Research on how expatriates adjust to their assignments, however, has been overwhelmingly conducted on Western ones, and their applicability to Chinese expatriates remains unclear. This chapter examines how expatriates in five European subsidiaries of large Chinese multinationals develop and use guanxi in the host country, and how this affects their adjustment. The findings contribute more generally to an understudied area of research on illuminating a variety of practices aimed at initiating, building, and utilizing guanxi in alien cultures.

Keywords Guanxi development process · CEs · Adjustment · U-curve theory

Introduction

Since Chinese organizations started to go global after the entry of China into the World Trade Organisation in 2001, a great number of Chinese

© The Author(s) 2019
B. X. Wang, *Guanxi in the Western Context*,
https://doi.org/10.1007/978-3-030-24001-1_4

multinational corporations (MNCs) have made significant investments worldwide. According to data gathered by Baker McKenzie (2018), in 2017 Europe attracted more Chinese investment in the West than did the USA, and Chinese MNCs closed deals worth $81 billion in Europe in that year. Consequently, this new phenomenon has stimulated Chinese nationals to become expatriate managers in Europe and to do business with Westerners (Li & Nuno Guimarães Costa, 2016; Lin, Zhao, & Lin, 2016). This new tendency does not appear to have attracted enough academic attention (Li & Nuno Guimarães Costa, 2016). Nevertheless, the comprehensive review by Takeuchi (2010) shows that although there is an enormous amount of research concerning expatriate adjustment, most studies focus on understanding the adjustment of Western managers sent to non-Western countries, including China (Braun & Warner, 2002; Selmer, 2010). Few studies have explored the inverse process. How CEs adjust in the host country, in particular, remains under-investigated.

Black, Mendenhall, and Oddou (1991) argued that relational skills are positively related to the degree of host-country adjustment, and the greater the expatriates' relational skills, the easier it is for them to interact with host nationals (Mendenhall & Oddou, 1985). As guanxi building is a key relational skill in the Chinese context, how this skill affects CEs' adjustment needs to be further studied. Therefore, this study is one of the first to explore the indigenous Chinese guanxi in the Western context by understanding guanxi building and its impact on the adjustment of CEs.

Wood and Mansour (2010) argued that expatriate adjustment is a multidimensional concept and follows a U-curve, and that guanxi provides an important framework for understanding CEs' interactions. Chen, Eberly, Chiang, Farh, and Cheng (2014) noted that there have been a number of theoretical models on the dynamic processes of guanxi building, maintenance, and use in a variety of fields such as management, marketing, and total quality management at the individual and organizational levels (Chen & Chen, 2004; Peng & Yang, 1999; Su, Mitchell, & Sirgy, 2007; Wong, Leung, Hung, & Ngai, 2007; Yau, Lee, Chow, Sin, & Tse, 2000). Scholars generally agree about the importance of guanxi building for both Chinese and foreign companies to do business in China (Bedford, 2011; Xin & Pearce, 1996; Yeung & Tung, 1996). However, there are a limited number of studies related to the process of guanxi building outside China.

My study analysed in depth how Europe-based CEs develop guanxi in the host country, with the purpose of furthering our understanding in this area of research by developing a process model of how guanxi is built at the interpersonal level in a Western context, and how it affects the adjustment of CEs. To examine these research questions, I conducted 25 in-depth interviews with CEs based in France, Germany, Luxemburg, Sweden, and the UK. Based on my observations, I identify the CEs' adjustment stages affected by their process of guanxi development.

In this chapter, I first review the existing literature about guanxi building and expatriate adjustment; next I explain how I collected and analysed the data and report findings from my analysis of the interviews. I then conclude by discussing these findings and alluding to the limitations of this exploratory research and its managerial implications. The contribution of this chapter is twofold: it is one of the first studies that applies and extends the guanxi-building process model, and it expands the stream of research on expatriate adjustment.

Guanxi Building

Mayfair Yang (2002) described guanxi building as the transformation process whereby two individuals construct a basis of familiarity to enable the subsequent development of a relationship. In this process, the gap between two hitherto unrelated individuals is bridged so that an outsider becomes part of the inner social circle of another person (Yeung & Tung, 1996). Scholars have confirmed that guanxi utilization significantly contributes to a firm's growth and success in the Chinese market (Gu, Hung, & Tse, 2008; Kotabe, Jiang, & Murray, 2008; Murray & Fu, 2016). Many scholars have explored the process of building, maintaining, and managing guanxi, showing how it is not only important for Chinese companies but also for Western ones operating in China (Chen, 2017; Chen & Chen, 2004; Leung, Wong, & Wong, 1996; Vanhonacker, 2004; Wong & Chan, 1999; Yeung & Tung, 1996).

Wong et al. (2007) explained the difference between Chinese guanxi and Western relationships: the Chinese approach focuses more on disciplined and cohesive values while Westerners emphasize fragmented societal values. Especially in China, gift giving has often been regarded as a major part of building guanxi. In the West, however, gift giving of significant economic value may often be viewed as illegal. As discussed in the previous chapters, Chinese values are rooted in the "rule of man", while Western societal values operate more on a "rule of law"; Chinese guanxi building is led by the "heart" while Western relationship building is managed by the "mind" (Wong et al., 2007).

Extensive research has investigated guanxi building in China among Chinese people and firms (Bu & Roy, 2015; Wong et al., 2007). In their study of Western firms in China, Murray and Fu (2016) found that some firms have a mechanism of internal guanxi to foster guanxi within their organizations. Internal guanxi-building processes involve interactions among employees at all levels that facilitate communication, clarify managerial expectations, and resolve ambiguities in employees' roles. Hence, many employees believe that good internal guanxi with one's managers reduces the uncertainty associated with performance evaluation; it therefore enhances employees' team morale, trust in managers, job satisfaction, and organizational commitment.

Chinese MNCs have increasingly invested in the West since the 2000s, and CEs have brought Chinese business culture to the host countries. As guanxi building is central to Chinese culture, how guanxi is utilized as an important vehicle of social communication and influence outside China is still under-researched (Lo, Chen, & Wilson, 2013). From 2000 to 2018, some findings about guanxi outside China emerged in 12 empirical papers, but only three of them focused on guanxi (Chen, 2017; Li & Nuno Guimarães Costa, 2016; Tan & Snell, 2002), and the other nine studies mentioned guanxi in passing but focused on either Chinese MNCs' strategy of outward foreign direct investment (Li & Nuno Guimarães Costa, 2016; Ramasamy, Yeung, & Laforet, 2012) or international assignment (IA) skills of Chinese expatriates (Lin, Li, & Roelfsema, 2018; Wang, Feng, Freeman, Fan, & Zhu, 2014; Wang, Freeman, & Zhu, 2013; Yao, 2014; Yao, Arrowsmith, & Thorn, 2016; Yao, Thorn, & Doherty, 2014; Yu, 2016). Most of these studies revealed that guanxi has an impact on the adjustment of CEs—as discussed next—but they also pointed out that further research was needed on how and to what extent.

Expatriate Adjustment

An expatriate's adjustment is defined as the degree of psychological comfort felt by an individual when he or she is sent to a foreign country (Black, 1988; Nicholson, 1984). The degree of adjustment is measured by variables such as comfort or satisfaction with the unfamiliar environment, attitudes, and contact with host nationals (Wood & Mansour, 2010). In the literature on international business and management, the success of MNCs is frequently linked to the work of expatriates sent by headquarters to ensure communication to subsidiaries. Expatriation should be a two-way interaction for both parties to learn from each other as well as to effectively bridge communication and maintain knowledge-sharing in a MNC (Lauring, 2011).

CEs

Expatriates from emerging Chinese MNCs partly differ from Western ones. Compared with their Western counterparts, less exposure to international businesses challenges CEs. The leadership behaviours among CEs can also be different in terms of the generation they belong to and their career experience. Most CEs belong to either the generation of the Cultural Revolution (i.e. they were born in the 1950s and 1960s) or that of the Social Reform (i.e. they were born in the 1970s), and each generation is characterized by its own distinct subculture. In terms of career experience, most CEs come from Chinese SOEs and private companies, with only a few of them from Western MNCs, with important consequences for their leadership behaviours.

Yao (2014) also suggested that while Western expatriates perceive IAs as valuable opportunities for professional and personal development, CEs perceive them more as job requirements. Their focus is to ensure the implementation and completion of allocated tasks given by their parent companies. The CEs are assigned by Chinese MNCs as the senior management for administrative, financial control, and technical requirements (Shen & Edwards, 2004). Many Chinese MNCs use CEs as a "control mechanism" to manage overseas subsidiaries and maintain a close fit with the Chinese parent company (Yao, 2014). Rather than being selected for their competence of leading a multinational team, most CEs are selected according to their loyalty to the parent company, as well as for being someone who can be trusted to obey the "order" unconditionally.

In Yao's (2014) research, CEs are not interested in getting familiar with the new society because their long-term career goals are in China. Preserving their Chinese identities is important for the strong connections with their families (most CEs part with their family members such as spouse and children during IAs) and organizations. This is in contrast to the Western expatriates who want to develop international competencies and global identities. Most CEs, instead, have strong desires to return to their familiar cultural context.

Zhong, Zhu, and Zhang (2015) identified 84 academic journal articles in English from 2001 to 2013 on the management issues of foreign expatriates in China and CEs working abroad. Of the 84, 72 focused on foreign expatriates working in China but only 12 on CEs working abroad. It is noticeable that the population of mainland CEs who take IAs has not been well represented; their adjustment has been significantly under-investigated in spite of the fact that China has become the second-largest source of outward foreign direct investment (Zhang, 2017).

Collectively, these studies highlight advantages and disadvantages of guanxi building in the Western context. Research shows, for instance, that Chinese firms have largely relied on guanxi before finalizing their investment decision; internalization advantages were only able to be realized when investing firms were good at utilizing guanxi. Guanxi may mitigate the transaction costs of acquiring strategic assets (Li-Ying, Stucchi, Visholm, & Jansen, 2013). Guanxi replication helps the Chinese parent companies in the definitions of their international expansion strategies (Li & Nuno Guimarães Costa, 2016). Guanxi building can be successful in developed markets, and Chinese firms can use guanxi when entering and expanding in developed markets, as well as in leveraging their existing guanxi with an overseas Chinese community to overcome the liability of being an outsider. However, its primary function shifts from initiating leads to retaining customers (Chen, 2017). Guanxi is a central factor for CEs to maintain or deepen connections with the home organization and develop contacts within a new organization (Yao et al., 2014). Good guanxi with managers and colleagues provides access to opportunities such as IAs and increases the chance of progression within the organization as well as expatriate selection and performance intervention (Yao et al., 2014).

The importance of guanxi has had an overall effect on the Chinese practices and processes of managing expatriates. CEs value guanxi over other factors such as skills and experiences in terms of their career progression. They perceive guanxi building as the work pressures in the early career stages (Yao, 2014). In particular, guanxi replication seems to be a viable and proper process that favours the adjustment of CEs in Western countries (e.g. Portugal) where they are open to the guanxi concept, which facilitates the guanxi replication process (Li & Nuno Guimarães Costa, 2016).

Research, however, also shows that guanxi building is very time-consuming. Chinese managers with Western education and/or with international experience of more than 10 years tend to successfully build guanxi with Americans, while those with less than five years of international experience perceive guanxi with Americans as a major challenge (Chua, Morris, & Ingram, 2009). Whether it is the similar pattern between Chinese managers and Europeans is understudied. Guanxi is often viewed as ignoring one's responsibility to host-country nationals (HCNs) in certain conditions in host countries (Wang et al., 2013). Guanxi skills applied by Chinese managers may not be suitable for meeting host-country expectations in foreign locations, and they cannot be transferred directly to cross-cultural contexts (Wang et al., 2014). Guanxi may not necessarily be accepted by the Westerner, which may result in conflicts, misunderstandings, and miscommunications (Yu, 2016). The development of guanxi affects expatriates with regard to how they are seen and judged by host nationals, which directly influences their performance as well as the evaluations by their bosses (Li & Nuno Guimarães Costa, 2016).

Despite the disadvantages mentioned above, it is clear from past studies that both Chinese firms and expatriates can benefit from proper guanxi building, and that this process is especially critical for the adjustment of CEs. So far, several studies have explored the impact of guanxi on the expatriation of Chinese managers in terms of their pre-IA as well as the connection and interaction with the parent company (Yao, 2014; Yao et al., 2014, 2016). Two papers have explored guanxi building by CEs with HCNs. One focused on the firm-level strategy (Chen, 2017). The other discussed guanxi replication and its impact on the adjustment of

CEs but only studied it in one host country of Europe—Portugal (Li & Nuno Guimarães Costa, 2016). Yu (2016) also argued that CEs faced a significant challenge in adjusting their ways of building and maintaining guanxi with host organization co-workers. Shi and Wang (2013) found that the main cause of culture shock for CEs is the differences between Chinese Confucianism and Western culture, such as communication and traditional issues. However, what specific Confucian culture and tradition cause culture shock has not been identified.

In this study, I explore how guanxi is developed in the West and how this process affects the adjustment of CEs.

A Process Model of Guanxi Building

Chen and Chen (2004) constructed a model of guanxi development to differentiate guanxi building into the three sequential stages of initiating, building, and using. At each stage, they examined three sets of variables: guanxi objectives, interactive activities, and operating principles. Guanxi objectives are to be reached through interactive activities of potential and actual guanxi parties, and operating principles underlie the interactive behaviours and moderate the relationship between these behaviours and guanxi objectives. The objectives are, at the guanxi initiation stage, to identify and create guanxi bases (objectives) through familiarization (interactive activities) based on mutual self-disclosure (operating principles); at the guanxi-building stage, to enhance guanxi quality (guanxi objectives) through expressive (affective trust) and instrumental (cognitive trust) interactions (interactive activities) based on dynamic reciprocity (operating principles); and at the guanxi using stage, to get benefits and adjust relational quality (objectives) through asking and giving favours (interactive activities) based on long-term equity (operating principles).

U-Curve Theory

Based on previous research, Black (1988) summarized four phases of expatriate adjustment as the U-curve. The first stage is referred to as a honeymoon stage. It occurs during the first few weeks after arrival, as the newly arrived expatriate is fascinated by the new and different aspects of the foreign culture and country. During this stage, the expatriate has not had sufficient time and experience in the host country to discover that many of his or her past habits and behaviours are inappropriate in the new culture. This lack of negative feedback and the newness of the foreign culture combine to produce the honeymoon effect. The second stage—culture shock—is identified by frustration and hostility towards the host country and its people when the newcomer begins to cope seriously with the real conditions of everyday life. This happens because the expatriate discovers that her or his past behaviours are inappropriate in the new culture and has received the maximum amount of negative feedback but as yet has not learned what to substitute in their stead. The third stage—adjustment—begins as the individual acquires some language skills and ability to move around on his or her own. In this stage, the expatriate begins to find a way of dealing with problems and also has developed some proficiency in adopting the new set of behaviours. Finally, in the mastery stage, the expatriate's adjustment is generally complete, and the incremental degree of adjustment is minimal. In this stage, the individual now knows and can properly assume the necessary behaviours to function effectively and without anxiety due to cultural differences.

Grounded in the process model of guanxi building (Chen & Chen, 2004) and U-curve theory (Black, 1988; Lysgaard, 1955), my qualitative study aimed at gaining a deeper understanding of how guanxi is developed in the West by CEs and how guanxi influences their adjustment experience while living in an international context.

Research Method

Research Setting

My study was conducted in international branches of Chinese MNCs in France, Germany, Luxemburg, Sweden, and the UK. This choice is justified by the fact that these host countries represent diverse cultures in developed markets in Europe. Also, the UK, France, and Germany are the first, third, and fourth recipients of Chinese investment from 2000 to 2015 (Zhang, 2016) and where a large number of CEs are located.

To ensure diversity, I interviewed CEs from different areas of business such as banking, telecommunications, aviation, energy, and the creative industry. The selected CEs had different experiences abroad: some of them had many years of international working experience while others had recently started their international careers. I included informants in different career positions, including senior executives, middle managers, and technical experts. However, all of them had at least two years of working experience in the chosen host countries. To successfully reach them, I used my guanxi combined with a snowball strategy. Table 4.1 lists detailed information on the informants.

Data Collection

I conducted 25 semi-structured interviews in this exploratory study. The interview protocol included open-ended questions to facilitate the collection of past and current experiences of the interviewees. To protect the identity of our informants, their names are coded across the study.

I interviewed the informants in their native language, Mandarin, for 40 to 90 minutes each, as detailed in Table 4.2. I asked informants to discuss their previous and current experiences as expatriates in their host countries, including their efforts to build guanxi and adapt to the new context. I included questions such as "Whether and how do you build your guanxi in the host country?" "Why do you develop guanxi in the host country?" and "What is your experience of adjustment in the new environment?" Interviews were recorded with the permission of the informants for later transcription. Five interviews were conducted via Skype due to geographical distance and availability issues. I imported the transcribed interviews into the qualitative analysis software Nvivo 11 as I collected them, and identified emerging themes as I worked through my sources. I adopted descriptive coding to pick reasonable evidences in the data as I read, and tagged them at the node section, then explored dimensions based on the characteristics of the informants. I also translated the transcripts into English to include as examples in the paper. I collected quantitative data,

Table 4.1 Informants

Informant ID	Host country	Gender	Years of IA	Months before culture shock
1	France	F	30	24
2	France	M	20	12
3	France	M	5	10
4	France	M	2	no
5	France	F	3	8
6	Germany	F	10	24
7	Germany	F	5	12
8	Germany	M	2	12
9	Germany	M	15	24
10	Germany	M	8	12
11	Luxembourg	M	20	24
12	Luxembourg	M	5	18
13	Luxembourg	F	20	12
14	Luxembourg	F	15	10
15	Luxembourg	F	2	no
16	Sweden	M	5	24
17	Sweden	M	8	12
18	Sweden	M	10	30
19	UK	F	6	12
20	UK	F	20	10
21	UK	M	15	12
22	UK	M	5	10
23	UK	F	5	12
24	UK	M	18	36
25	UK	M	13	96
				18.24

indicated on Table 4.1, in terms of the timing when the informant experienced frustration during adjustment (i.e. culture shock); then I depicted the CE's adjustment stage, illustrated in Fig. 4.4, according to the mean value of 18.24 months, which will be discussed when I later present the process model.

Data Analysis

I analysed these data employing grounded theory building to code and develop concepts, categories, and themes which became the basis for the-

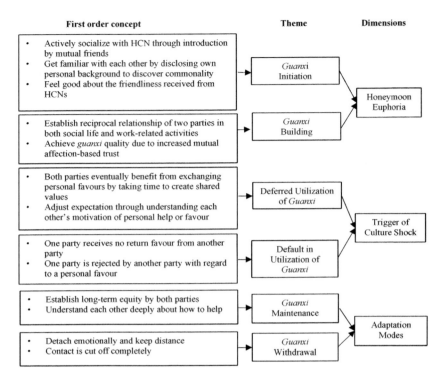

Fig. 4.1 Data structure

ory. I broke down data into substantive codes in a line-by-line manner and compared incidents with one another for similarities and differences until the core category for the process of guanxi building and expatriate adjustment was merged. I conducted selective coding by employing guanxi building and U-curve theories to build up substantive codes into a substantive theory. The final data structure is illustrated in Fig. 4.1, which summarizes the second-order themes on which I built the process model of guanxi building along with the expatriate adjustment stages.

Findings

As illustrated in Fig. 4.1, there are three main dimensions to the model of how guanxi development affects the adjustment of CEs: (1) honeymoon euphoria, (2) trigger of culture shock, and (3) adaptation modes. It reveals that the stages of guanxi initiation and guanxi building are in line with the honeymoon phase of expatriate adjustment. Their experience in the stage of guanxi utilization triggers culture shock, which causes them to adopt one of two adaptation modes: continue using and maintaining guanxi as a result of the deferred utilization of guanxi; or withdraw guanxi building due to the default utilization of guanxi and shift to the Western way of interacting with HCNs. Table 4.2 illustrates the data supporting interpretation of this model.

Honeymoon Euphoria

All informants expressed their excitement when they received the IA in Europe. In addition to Western expatriates' fascination with what was new and different in the foreign culture and country, CEs also perceived the assignment in the West as a privilege and an expression of enormous trust granted by the parent company. In particular, they considered this a great opportunity to improve themselves through learning from the advanced West, rather than sharing or teaching best practices to a developed market, which is the main objective and mentality of the Western expatriates. Therefore, during this stage, CEs actively became involved in and initiated many activities through the people they knew in China or HCN colleagues at work. Coming from the deep-rooted guanxi culture in China, CEs normally initiated guanxi without realizing it.

Guanxi initiation. In line with previous research (Chen & Chen, 2004), this research shows that CEs took the initiative to interact with HCNs, in the following ways.

Actively socialize with HCNs through introduction by mutual friends. Before moving to the host country, in addition to attending pre-IA orientations arranged by the parent company, most CEs asked friends in China to make introductions for them to build potential guanxi in the host country. This reflects the fact that Chinese prefer to make new friends through recommendations by mutual friends rather than "cold-calling", due to the prime motivation of affect-trust.

> I was very excited to get this opportunity working in the UK. I used to read a lot of English novels when I was in university, and I admire British history and culture. My friends in China have introduced me to their friends in the UK. During the first three months, I attended many parties after work and have known several local Chinese and British people. They were all very nice to me and I felt very welcome. People in the UK are very polite and helpful. I feel there is a lot commonality between Chinese and British. Also, comparing with where I come from in China, London is very clean and convenient. I was very happy to have this opportunity working here. (Informant 19)

Get familiar with each other by disclosing one's own personal background to discover commonality. In contrast to the cautiousness or emphasis on privacy in the West, CEs were very open about personal matters. In particular, this was the way to build trust and test the waters of further action of guanxi building.

> I was introduced to a local potential business partner. I suggested to meet him in a café where we can feel relaxed to connect. He looked quite serious or maybe professional at the beginning, I then started to tell him my personal background and story, and actually, I did not talk about business at all in our first meeting. He might think I was odd, but after a while, he shared his background and personal story with me. Then, we realized that we are all football fan of FC Bayern Munich. (Informant 6)

Feel good about the friendliness received from HCNs. CEs regarded the politeness and friendliness as the same thing. Chinese can be quite reserved to strangers in official gatherings or business-related social networking but can be very warm and friendly to strangers in a gathering of friends or family. The Western politeness at the first meeting was perceived as surprising friendliness by CEs.

> When I started this job, I was overwhelmed by my local colleagues and even people on the streets, they were super friendly. Once, I lost my way home,

an elegant old lady took me back. I attended many gatherings, wherever I go, people are so nice. I didn't miss home at all. (Informant 5)

In this stage, CEs were very open in meeting new people and gaining new experiences to familiarize themselves with the protocols of the host country.

Guanxi building. Having familiarized themselves with and opened up to each other in the stage of guanxi initiation, most CEs began to evaluate the new relationship with regard to whether there was mutual benefit in terms of both expressive and instrumental transactions. Then they made an effort with the target party to increase mutual trust and affection by sharing personal emotions, organizing family events, and offering their help to the degree that they could deliver it without difficulty. If the other party received it well and also reciprocated, the foundation of guanxi between two parties in both social life and work-related activities was created.

Establish reciprocal relationship of two parties in both social life and work-related activities. Due to the blurred boundary between social and business life in Chinese society, CEs expected mutual reciprocity with their guanxi counterparts at all aspects in life.

I like this country and I wanted to make friend with local nationals as I am far away from home, I might need help although my company provides strong support. I made a local friend, I felt so easy to connect with him because he is very interested in Chinese culture. I also felt that he was trustworthy. We invited each other to our homes. I cooked Chinese food for him and he cooked spaghetti for me. Every time when I come back from China, I would get some souvenirs for his children. He recommended a local school for my daughter. I believe we can help each other if we need to sort out some issues. (Informant 14)

Achieve guanxi quality due to increased mutual affection-based trust. CEs believed that guanxi quality was enhanced by deepening emotional connection, as the mutual trust was achieved through affection first.

We became very close friend quickly after we met in a social event organized by the company. She is a very warm person and we got along very well. We went out for dinner or shopping periodically. We trust each other very much like sisters. We can share personal story and feelings easily. (Informant 5)

Trigger of Culture Shock

As explained earlier, unlike Western expatriates, the timing for CEs to experience the culture shock varies from months to years; according to the informants, this mainly depends on their experiences in the stages of guanxi utilization. This study reveals that they felt frustration and hostility towards the host-country nationals when they discovered that their guanxi utilization behaviour was inappropriate in the new culture, and the difference between reality and their expectations was enormous.

In the guanxi utilization stage, two parties had reached a high quality of guanxi through trust at both the cognitive and affective levels, and they were ready to exchange favours and establish long-term equity. However, in the Western context, two consequences of guanxi utilization triggered CEs' culture shock. First, it may be that the personal favour was not offered at the time that one party expected but was delivered later due to different understandings of guanxi utilization by both parties (deferred utilization). Second, the personal favour may not be delivered as one party expected at all (default in utilization).

Deferred utilization. The ultimate goal of guanxi is favour exchange, reciprocity, loyalty, and obligation (Chen & Chen, 2004). At the stage of guanxi utilization, both parties have benefited from exchanging personal favours, and it is the moment of truth to prove the adage that "a friend in need is a friend indeed". Among the 25 informants, 10 of them managed to use their guanxi successfully to get personal benefits, but they also experienced culture shock because of the long and winding road they had been through.

Both parties eventually benefit from exchanging personal favours by taking time to create shared values. Fulfilling a personal favour was the touchstone for CEs in their guanxi dynamics, which revealed the fundamental values CEs and their guanxi counterparts sustain. However, a guanxi process cannot be completed without the success of personal favour exchange; therefore, CEs were willing to make more efforts.

We are not only business partners. We became very close friends 10 years ago, and our families go out together as well. His family stayed with us when they came to China for a holiday. He is senior than I am in the organisation, but we work in different business. However, when I applied for a senior position, as a member of the panel, he did not vote for me. I did not get the job and was very disappointed and shocked with his behaviour. He explained to me that I was not suited for the job, but he is my friend and he should have supported me. Anyway, later, he recommended me for another position, which is also a kind of promotion. I was the one who got the job among the three candidates due to his support. I am grateful, but his first reaction really hurt me. (Informant 9)

Adjust expectation through understanding each other's motivation of personal help or favour. It was a shared view that building guanxi requires patience and deep understanding of each other's motives and needs. Given the vast cultural distance, some CEs were quite tolerant towards their HCNs' guanxi counterparts and willing to reflect and flexible in enabling personal favour exchange in one way or another.

I recruited my business partner five years ago, I like him because he is very smart. I spent a lot of time to develop him over past few years, and I also care about him as a brother and tried not asking him to work over the weekends which is quite normal in our company. We have good guanxi. He sees me his mentor and friend. However, he left the job a couple of months ago when it was the critical time during the annual audit, and he was the only person understanding the whole protocols. I relied on him completely. He said sorry and sent me a thanks letter to express his gratitude, but he declined my request of helping me for four more months. He said that this was just a job but not a private matter, anyone at work should be replaceable, it did not help myself by relying on him so much. He recommended another person to me to take his task. Initially, I was very resentful and hurt, I really took it personally. Then I cut off from him for a couple of months and turned down his invite for a drink in the bar after work. By the time the audit was completed, the person he recommended did fair job. I realized that he was right, I should develop a team rather my favourite person, also I should not have taken it personally about his leaving. Anyway, I eventually contacted him and now, we are not colleagues anymore, but real friends. (Informant 10)

In both cases above, although the guanxi practices of Informants 9 and 10 eventually did them a favour, their initial actions almost damaged their years of building guanxi, which triggered culture shock because they could not understand why their guanxi parties did not help when they needed. Given the "rule of man" culture, the affection-based personal support among guanxi parties is expected to be superior to business ethics. The "touchstone" nature of a personal request is probably made unconsciously among Chinese; however, the Europeans might consider it unethical.

Default in utilization. This is the stage in which one or two parties eventually failed to use guanxi and the personal relationship was damaged or ended.

One party receives no return favour from another party. CEs took the initiative to offer favours in order to receive favours in need and perceived the shared understanding without explicit communication with their counterparts. However, HCNs were not able to capture CEs' intention or nuance:

> It took us two years to develop a good guanxi as business partners, although she is French, she likes Chinese culture and I like French culture. I trusted her a lot. As she doesn't understand Chinese, in two years, I helped her a lot at work to translate for her as we have many documents written in Chinese, as well Chinese colleagues speak Chinese in the office. I thought she would have appreciated and helped me as well. However, I was very disappointed that she never helped. For instance, I often organize the visit for the headquarter delegation during the weekend, and I hoped that she could have helped take them out as she knows this city very well and I even don't speak French properly, she always said she will try her best and then she gave me some reasons about something happen at home. Now, I have detached from her and I don't trust her anymore. (Informant 1)

One party is rejected by another party with regard to a personal favour. Indirectness or subtle and gentle demeanour to maintain face for all parties is one of the Confucian codes of conduct. Failing to help a guanxi party because of uncontrollable variables can put one in debt, but direct rejection of a favour to the guanxi party was perceived by CEs as a deadly sin due to the breach of the psychological contract as well as the huge face loss.

He is one of my business partners in the UK. We got along well and shared a lot of information and affection. He introduced me to the pub culture, and we enjoyed having beer together periodically. I introduced him to Chinese food and tea. We shared leisure time together. In eight years, I trusted him very much and saw him my close friend and my good guanxi in the UK. However, when the local authority questioned our project in terms of ethical issues, he did not help me at all and detached himself from me. I could not believe it. I felt extremely hurt and resentful and also realized that he is very selfish and a cold-hearted hypocrite. Ever since, I am very cautious when dealing with local people and have initiated guanxi with nobody. (Informant 20)

In line with previous research (Chen, 2017), to the Chinese, affection is the first step in building guanxi with strangers, which is an emotional connection through mutual friends. When managed well, this guanxi further establishes cognitive and affection-based trust, which is prerequisite for long-term guanxi filled with constant personal favour exchanges. Therefore, when CEs perceived that guanxi was established and ready for utilization, the failure of delivery by another party would make CEs feel hurt emotionally, then confused mentally. However, in Europe, the sense of legality, ethics, and fairness properly exceeds personal affection and sense of personal obligation.

In addition, most experiences of guanxi development shared by the informants were their interactions with HCNs. Few of them also shared unsuccessful experiences with non-colleague HCC; however, these experiences did not trigger their cultural shock because both parties could realize at the guanxi initiation stage that they could not resonate at a deep emotional level or have a feeling of trust, and they stopped the process tacitly without making offence. This is mainly due to the same cultural background and psychological make-up that both parties possessed, which can be perceived.

She is a mutual friend of my friend in China, she has lived this country for more than 10 years, she took me out for a lunch when I just arrived as my friend in China asked her to "look after" me. We had a pleasant chat; however, I didn't feel we could connect in deep level. She seems very Westernize and detached, a bit "cold" or too professional. Anyway, although we are all Chinese living abroad, I don't think we can establish real guanxi. We communicated via WeChat occasionally and stopped naturally after a while. This is quite common in China as well if you don't feel connected with someone. (Informant 23)

It seems that guanxi building ended after one unsuccessful attempt; actually, this "attempt" is often at the expected "payback time" by one guanxi party for his/her accumulated efforts for years.

Adaptation Modes

Having coped with culture shock during the stage of guanxi utilization, CEs began to take one of two ways of dealing with problems, as well as to develop some proficiency in adopting the new set of behaviours in order to adjust.

Guanxi maintenance. This is based on the success of an exchange of personal favours when two parties have established deeper trust at both the cognitive and affective levels. CEs have learned to modify their expectations of the ways of using guanxi in the West.

Establish long-term equity by both parties. The most important benefit for CEs to build guanxi was the reciprocity in the long run. They maintained guanxi on a regular basis by exchanging affections and favours as they expected a long-term return in investment.

I have lived here for 20 years. It took me quite a long time to establish close guanxi with one of my local friends. She is my former colleague. At the beginning, I was very Chinese, expecting her to help me in my way. After several occasions, I realized that I needed to win her trust by demonstrating how capable I was at work. I did a great job establishing an internal audit process, which helped the company gain a certificate from the local authority. Since then, she openly expressed her admiration about my achievement and we became good friends. I provided some tips to her of how to work in a Chinese company, and she helped me polish my English for my PhD book and find a great school for my daughter. I am sure we are life-long friends and will help each other forever. (Informant 11)

The case of Informant 11 suggests that guanxi can be developed in the West; however, as noted by Chen (2017), CEs need to build cognition-based trust before affection-based trust. The second case suggests that cross-cultural understanding is critical to manage expectations and reduce bias towards alien culture.

Understand each other deeply about how to help. Given the cultural distance between CEs and HCNs, they had different ways to help each other, which sometimes were perceived as sabotage by CEs. Even among Chinese, misunderstanding occurs often in a newly established guanxi. Fully and deeply understanding each other requires both parties to make efforts to avoid the common problem of the road to hell being paved with good intentions.

> I have lived and work here for 15 years and gone through hard time at first four years. I was a very traditional Chinese senior manager behaving like a big sister or mother and tried to make local business partners work together like a family member. Then, I realized that the local people are quite self-reserved and private. I tried to invite some of them for tea and coffee at my home, and I failed several times. I thought they did not like me, but some of them really helped me at work and I have achieved because of their contribution. Then, I understood that Westerner set quite clear boundary between work and private life. I have very good guanxi with my two local friends who are my former colleagues and we still meet and help each other in many ways. (Informant 15)

Guanxi withdrawal. In adapting to the failure of guanxi utilization, CEs detached emotionally and kept a distance from their guanxi parties. Therefore, guanxi quality deteriorated progressively, and contact was cut off completely. After a while, they adjusted and adopted host-country social behaviours.

Detach emotionally and keep distance. Open disagreement or break-up is considered the worst manners in any relationship. If it was not a matter of life or death, due to the face culture CEs chose to withdraw rather than confront when in conflict.

> I was very disappointed and hurt for a while after my so-called best friend gave the business to another agent but me in his own rationale. However, I

Table 4.2 Data supporting interpretation of guanxi development affecting expatriates' adjustment

Theme	Representative quotations
Guanxi initiation	*Honeymoon euphoria*
	I was very excited to work in Europe. My classmate in the university has worked here for a few years. He introduced me to some local people, and I went out with them quite often as I was very curious about their work and lifestyle in this country. (Informant 2)
	We get along very well although we come from different cultures. I don't think there is much difference between us in terms of the way we feel about relationships. We visited each other's homes and shared jokes and personal stories. (Informant 4)
	The local people are very warm, and I felt so welcomed, which was much better than I expected as I was told in China that Westerners lack human touch. One of my local colleagues invited me to her home and she has a lovely family. (Informant 8)
	The local culture is not that different from China; people like to get together talking about family and personal matters. I felt not alien at all. Our local business partners invited us out for drinks like we did in China. (Informant 10)
Guanxi building	He is very kind and helped me at both work and family settle down. I also helped him get promoted. Be honest, he deserved it as he's very capable. (Informant 1)
	We helped each other at work as she knows the local regulations and I know the Chinese company's policy. We are like sisters, we are of similar ages and we both have sons. Anyway, I see her as my friend, not only a business partner. (Informant 5)
	We actually shared a lot in common and trust each other. He always praised me how capable I am in my job, and I always praise him about his knowledge about Chinese culture. I am very impressed with his savvy about Chinese history and culture. (Informant 3)
	He comes across hard, but he has a good heart. We used to argue about the way we implementing the policy assigned by the Chinese company. At the beginning, I thought he did not want to follow up. After he took so much time to explain to me the local protocol and my personal experience of working here, I started to appreciate how helpful he was. I really rely on him to handle the business in this country as I trust him very much; our guanxi is very close. (Informant 17)

(continued)

Table 4.2 (continued)

Theme	Representative quotations
	Trigger of culture shock
Deferred utilization of guanxi	My relationship with Andrew went through ups and downs. A couple of years ago, we almost fell over because he did not help me when I needed him to collect my daughter from the airport when I was in China because he was busy at work, although he apologized. I thought that any good friend would do it in China. Anyway, later on, he helped my daughter get into a very good school in this country; I am very pleased and grateful. (Informant 18)
	I really need this business to make my boss happy in China, Tom was the decision maker of my client, and I have known Tom since he worked in China 10 years ago. I could not believe that he did not give that business to me; instead, he recommended me to another potential client who was happy with our product. Still, I was very disappointed at the time. (Informant 6)
Default in utilization of guanxi	I was very shocked and angry when he rejected my request of his help on introducing me to a local authority in order to get approval of our business project in this country, which is critical for the company and my career. I used to help him by praising him to my boss in China as I really see him as a friend. I said to him that in China, true friends would try whatever they can to help each other, and he just simply said that he had to follow the local rules and ethics, and he was sorry he could not help much. To me, this is just an excuse! (Informant 7)
	Over the past few years, I tried my best to help her such as arranging Chinese class for her and got my friend in China to look after her family when they had holiday in China. However, I have not received any return favour from her apart from verbal thanks, and I realize that she takes my friendship for granted. (Informant 16)
	I helped his son get an internship in China a few years ago. However, when I asked him to get internships for my daughter in this country, he could not deliver it because he did not try hard. I am very disappointed and hurt. (Informant 15)

(continued)

Table 4.2 (continued)

Theme	Representative quotations
	Adaptation modes
Guanxi maintenance	I am very glad that I have a very good friend in this country; we trust each other very very much. I believe that we will try our best to help each other in many ways. It took a long time to establish this close guanxi outside China, but all efforts are worthwhile. I feel safe living here because of this guanxi. (Informant 12)
	I am lucky that we became buddies after we went through cultural misunderstanding in the past. I was not aware how different we perceive personal relationships; he prefers "right", and I prefer "reasonable". Anyway, we have reached the stage that we trust each other deeply and we exchange favours without compromising our own preferences. (Informant 21)
	After 10 years, we really know each other very well; particularly, we know how to help each other. I would help her in Western way which ensures her the legality of what I am doing, and she would help me in Chinese way, which makes me feel I can share my emotions with her at any time. (Informant 23)
Guanxi withdrawal	I was really hurt when my so-called friend refused to help me when I needed him to defend me against the accusation from another business partner about my careless preparing of an audit document. He knew how much effort I had made on this initiative. I have recovered and realized that local people lack human sense; this is their culture, which is very different from Chinese culture. I have learned to detach and interact with local people in their own way, which is not very difficult for me. (Informant 22)
	I thought we had established good guanxi until the moment I could not get his support on my project. He said that he was not capable, but I believe that he did not want to help. Anyway, I understand that he wants to spend more time with his family but not friends. I have accepted and moved on without practicing guanxi with him anymore. (Informant 24)
	I learned my lesson that we have fundamental cultural difference with Westerners. They are rational and logical, and we are emotional and relational. Having gone through culture shock of getting no help from my local "friend", I have stopped developing guanxi but to behave like host country national to conduct normal social networking without much personal expectation. Now, I am getting used to this culture. (Informant 25)

eventually let it go, accepted the fact that he is not Chinese, and will never understand what he has done to me. I did not argue with him. Instead, I detached and kept the emotions to myself. Since then, I have maintained a professional relationship with him just like typical working partners' relationship in the West. Now, I do not expect to build guanxi in this country, and I am fine with it. I actually live a much simpler life outside China and I start to enjoy it. (Informant 7)

Contact is cut off completely and one moves on. In the worst scenario, when CEs felt betrayed by the guanxi counterpart, they chose to give up, although with great difficulty, by justifying that cultural difference was too significant to overcome.

I tried to build guanxi in this country when I joined this subsidiary. However, I had a bad experience that I trusted one local person very much, I introduced him to my guanxi in China to do business. He got into China market and never involved me. I cut off with him completely. Anyway, I learned my lesson, ever since, I have followed the local protocol to socialize with people but no more guanxi practice. I feel quite comfortable now. (Informant 21)

Building guanxi in China is properly the most natural thing for CEs; nevertheless, the challenge of using guanxi is widely recognized, given the constant change in terms of policy and regulation, personnel mobility, and social transformation. Thus, most CEs are flexible and skilful in managing their expectations when using guanxi under different circumstances. Subsequently, most CEs have managed to adapt to the host country during their expatriation, though this has typically taken a long period of time.

A Process Model of Guanxi Development and the Adjustments of Chinese Expatriates

In the previous section, I reported a narrative description of the guanxi development by CEs in the host country and how the process evolved over time. In this section, I present a process model (visualized in Fig. 4.2) that builds on my analysis to theorize how guanxi development affects the adjustments of CEs. This model builds on two theoretical

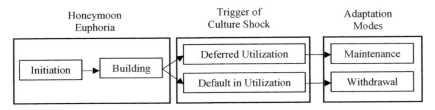

Fig. 4.2 A process model of guanxi development and the adjustment of Chinese expatriates

frameworks—the U-curve adjustment and the guanxi-building process—which I introduced earlier.

My findings suggest a strong relationship between the adjustment stage of CEs and their guanxi development stage. In the first stage of adjustment (honeymoon euphoria), although CEs are aware of the different environmental culture, unconsciously they carry on what they normally do in China. Given their excellent guanxi-building skill, which helped them get an IA opportunity in Europe, they quickly start the process to develop guanxi (guanxi initiation), set up a guanxi base, and interact with local people to familiarize themselves with guanxi candidates through mutual self-disclosure. Being prepared for a time-consuming process, CEs tend to take time to understand the candidate rather than rush into the next stage. When CEs have good feelings about the candidate, they make an effort to enhance guanxi quality (guanxi building) by sharing affection and work-related tasks through reciprocal activities.

CEs are still in the honeymoon stage while going through two stages of guanxi development. My observations suggest that the experience of using guanxi (guanxi utilization) triggers CEs' culture shock (trigger of culture shock). Two situations are observed at this stage: some CEs encounter unexpected reluctance from a guanxi party, but eventually get benefit by exchanging favours, and establish long-term guanxi in a delayed fashion (deferred utilization); other CEs encounter unexpected resistance from a guanxi party and fail to get benefit and exchange favours (default in utilization).

Either of these two experiences triggers culture shock in the process of CEs' adjustment. This leads to two actions of guanxi development

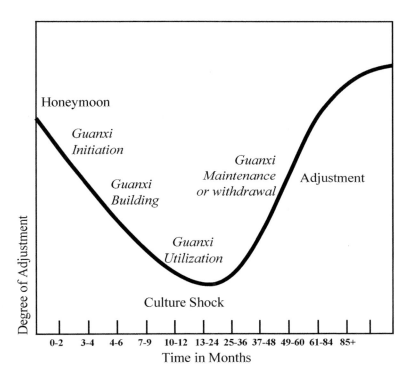

Fig. 4.3 V-curve adjustment

in the stage of adaption (adaptation mode): having experienced deferred utilization, the CE re-evaluates guanxi quality, adjusts expectations, and maintains long-term equity (maintenance); or, having experienced default in utilization, the CE gives up guanxi development and detaches from the guanxi party (withdrawal).

The honeymoon phase for 25 CEs, including stages of guanxi initiation and building, lasted from six months to eight years (see Table 4.1), and two of them had not experienced culture shock at the time of the interview. The mean value was 18.4 months, depicted as a V-curve in Fig. 4.3.

Discussion and Conclusion

This is one of the first studies to apply and extend the guanxi-building process model abroad. My findings indicate that guanxi development abroad differs from guanxi development in China in three respects.

First, the process is more complicated, as it intertwines with the expatriate adjustment process. The guanxi initiation and building stages might be longer than in China, as the excitement of a new post and the perception of overwhelming friendliness from HCNs during the honeymoon stage can be misleading. Consequently, CEs are more enthusiastic in taking more time and effort than they usually do in China to build guanxi with HCNs, and they think it is normal to encounter reluctance or resistance from HCNs as it happens in China during the process of building guanxi, which delays their feeling of culture shock. Thus, the honeymoon stage of CEs is also longer than for Western CEs.

Second, shared value between guanxi parties determines the success of guanxi development. In China, it is recognized by both parties at the first stage of guanxi development (i.e. initiation), but given the different institutional and social context in the West, it challenges both parties, and the personal value tends to be realized at the utilization stage, when both parties have invested a great deal. Thus, if each other's values do not resonate, the relationship is impaired.

Third, I identify the specific stage (utilization) of guanxi development outside China where the cross-cultural misunderstanding and conflict occur. Along with the increasing time and effort that CEs spend in the first two stages, their expectation for HCNs to use guanxi for personal favour exchange is automatically increased. However, the tacit nature of guanxi building (Bian, 2017) might be completely miscomprehended by HCNs as the Western friendliness to CEs. Hence, the contrast of disappointment over favour exchange failure and high expectation of guanxi utilization is too large to tackle, which causes conflict between CEs and HCNs and triggers culture shock for CEs.

My study also expands the stream of research on expatriate adjustment in two respects. First, previous research based on Western expatriates has noted that good relational skills help expatriate adjustment (Black, 1988; Black & Mendenhall, 1991); in contrast, CEs who benefit from their own

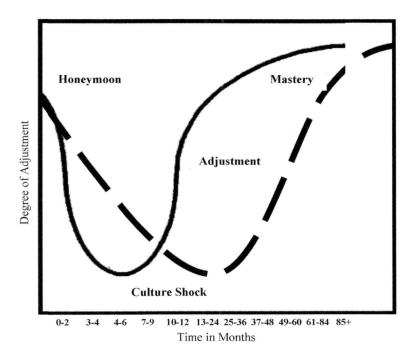

Fig. 4.4 U-curve vs. V-curve

superior relational skills in gaining an IA opportunity suffer culture shock due to developing guanxi with HCNs. Therefore, it reveals the distinction at the personal value between Western social networking or interpersonal relationships and Chinese guanxi.

Second, research on Western expatriates shows that they normally start to feel culture shock after three months, indicated as a U-curve (Black, 1988; Black & Mendenhall, 1991). However, the CEs I interviewed took from six months to eight years. Their honeymoon stage, depicted by the dotted line in Fig. 4.4, is therefore much longer than for their Western counterparts. This result shows that guanxi development alters the usual timing of the adjustment curve.

Given the pervasive nature of guanxi in Chinese society as part of deep-rooted national culture, CEs have brought not only business but also guanxi to the West. This research on perceived cultural distance between

China and the five European countries (Hofstede, 2001) reveals that most CEs experimented with guanxi building almost unconsciously in the early stage of their expatriation. Constricted by the time-consuming character of guanxi building, CEs tended to be more patient and tolerant when they interacted with HCNs, which prolonged the honeymoon euphoria during their adjustment. Most CEs were aware that it is time-consuming to develop guanxi; nevertheless, it is a personal investment in time, emotion, and money—in particular in the host country, where there is a lack of a guanxi base such as family and kinship. Therefore, they were quite selective with regard to the guanxi candidates and tended to be cautious about taking the next step after the guanxi initiation stage, as they would like to ensure long-term equity.

Among all informants, no CE returned to China because of maladaptation, but they eventually did so because of job rotation or promotion. This actually reflects the flexibility and pragmatism of Chinese culture, as it enables CEs to overcome the culture shock as long as they are aware of the cultural difference between Chinese guanxi grounded in affection at the emotional level and Western social networking anchored in cognition at the rational level.

Concerning managerial implications, this chapter provides some insights and guidelines towards guanxi development outside China and its impact on the process of adjustment of CEs in the Western context. Two suggestions for Chinese MNCs, SOEs in particular, come out of this research.

The first suggestion is to establish an organizational culture to underpin the globalization strategy, which is embedded in national cultures but opens to diversity and embraces multicultural values, such as in the Tang dynasty, a thousand years ago, at the heyday of multicultural integration in China, when the values of Confucianism, Daoism, Buddhism, and Christianity were allowed to coexist. Then, strategize guanxi development to adapt to the values and norms of the host country. The affection trait of guanxi is well received in the West due to human nature. However, given the top-down culture in Chinse MNCs, this culture needs to be enabled by the top management at the board level, who must have business vision and insight from the global perspective, not just political savvy.

The second suggestion is to redefine the HRM strategy by selecting, developing, and deploying cross-cultural talents who are from various cultural backgrounds, not limited to Chinese. The criteria for expatriates' selection should emphasize cross-cultural competency, emotional and cultural intelligence, and international communication skills in addition to language proficiency. Moreover, the company should provide systematic pre-IA training for CEs to help expatriates go through the adjustment stage by improving their understanding of cross-cultural differences in the business, social, and legal domains, and raising their self-efficacy and perception skills towards alien cultures before sending them abroad.

Limitation

Although this exploratory study opens up interesting prospects for future research concerning guanxi building in Western countries, it did not examine how HCNs perceive guanxi building and the level of their acceptance. Further research could also advance this exploratory study by testing the model of guanxi development and the V-curve relationship. It would certainly be important to understand how guanxi can be developed effectively across cultures to facilitate the process of CEs' adjustment as well as the local acceptance of Chinese MNCs. Furthermore, all informants have worked for large Chinese MNCs, which provides them with a strong sense of security during IAs that might help them a great deal in going through their adjustment. Therefore, future research could explore how CEs from small- and medium-sized companies make their own adjustments.

References

Bedford, O. (2011). Guanxi-building in the workplace: A dynamic process model of working and backdoor guanxi. *Journal of Business Ethics, 104*(1), 149–158.

Bian, Y. (2017). The comparative significance of guanxi. *Management and Organisation Review, 13*(02), 261–267.

Black, J. S. (1988). Work role transitions: A study of American expatriate managers in Japan. *Journal of International Business Studies, 19*(2), 277–294.

Black, J. S., & Mendenhall, M. (1991). The U-curve adjustment hypobook revisited: A review and theoretical framework. *Journal of International Business Studies, 22*(2), 225–247.

Black, J. S., Mendenhall, M., & Oddou, G. (1991). Toward a comprehensive model of international adjustment: An integration of multiple. *The Academy of Management Review, 16*(2), 291–317.

Braun, W. H., & Warner, M. (2002). Strategic human resource management in Western multinationals in China: The differentiation of practices across different ownership forms. *Personnel Review, 31*(5), 553–579.

Bu, N., & Roy, J. P. (2015). Guanxi practice and quality: A comparative analysis of Chinese managers' business-to-business and business-to-government ties. *Management and Organisation Review, 11*(2), 263–287.

Chen, J. (2017). Internationalization of Chinese firms: What role does guanxi play for overcoming their liability of outsidership in developed markets? *Thunderbird International Business Review, 59*(3), 367–383.

Chen, X.-P., & Chen, C. C. (2004). On the intricacies of the Chinese guanxi: A process model of guanxi development. *Asia Pacific Journal of Management, 21*(3), 305–324.

Chen, X.-P., Eberly, M. B., Chiang, T. J., Farh, J. L., & Cheng, B. S. (2014). Affective trust in Chinese leaders: Linking paternalistic leadership to employee performance. *Journal of Management, 40*(3), 796–819.

Chua, R. Y. J., Morris, M. W., & Ingram, P. (2009). Guanxi vs networking: Distinctive configurations of affect- and cognition-based trust in the networks of Chinese vs American managers. *Journal of International Business Studies, 40*(3), 490–508.

Gu, F. F., Hung, K., & Tse, D. K. (2008). When does guanxi matter? Issues of capitalization and its dark sides. *Journal of Marketing, 72*(3), 12–28.

Hofstede, G. (2001). *Culture's consequences* (2nd ed.). London, UK: Sage.

Kotabe, M., Jiang, C. X., & Murray, J. Y. (2008). Institutional relatedness, resources acquisition, and performance outcomes of Chinese multinational companies. *Academy of Management Best Paper Proceedings*, 1–6.

Lauring, J. (2011). Intercultural organisational communication: The social organizing of interaction in international encounters. *Journal of Business Communication, 48*(3), 231–255.

Leung, T. K. P., Wong, Y. H., & Wong, S. (1996). A study of Hong Kong businessmen's perceptions of the role of guanxi in the People's Republic of China. *Journal of Business Ethics, 15*(7), 749–758.

Li, J., & Nuno Guimarães Costa, P. N. (2016). Chinese expatriates' adjustment process in Portugal: On the road to guanxi replication. *Management Research: Journal of the Iberoamerican Academy of Management, 14*(2), 166–187.

Lin, L., Li, P. P., & Roelfsema, H. (2018). The traditional Chinese philosophies in inter-cultural leadership. *Cross Cultural & Strategic Management,* CCSM-01-2017-0001.

Lin, Z., Zhao, Z., & Lin, Z. (2016). Culture, expatriation and performance: Case of Chinese multinational enterprises. *Chinese Management Studies, 10*(2), 346–364.

Li-Ying, J., Stucchi, T., Visholm, A., & Jansen, J. S. (2013). Chinese multinationals in Denmark: Testing the eclectic framework and internalization theory. *Multinational Business Review, 21*(1), 65–86.

Lo, K., Chen, S., & Wilson, M. (2013). *Guanxi* in organizations: Cross-cultural perspectives on an enduring construct. In R. L. Morrison & H. D. Cooper-Thomas (Eds.), *Relationships in organizations.* London: Palgrave Macmillan.

Lysgaard, S. (1955). Adjustment in a foreign society: Norwegian Fulbright grantees visiting the United States. *International Social Science Bulletin, 7,* 45–105.

McKenzie, B. (2018). *Rising tension: Assessing China's FDI dropping in Europe and North America.* Rhodium Group.

Mendenhall, M., & Oddou, G. (1985). The dimensions of acculturation: Expatriate. *Academy of Management Review, 10*(1), 39–47.

Murray, J. Y., & Fu, F. Q. (2016). Strategic guanxi orientation: How to manage distribution channels in China? *Journal of International Management, 22*(1), 1–16.

Nicholson, N. (1984). A theory of work role transitions. *Administrative Science Quarterly, 29,* 172–191.

Peng, S. [彭泗清], & Yang, Z. [杨中芳]. (1999). Impact factors and development process of interpersonal relationship [人际交往关系的影响因素与发展过程]. *Indigenous Psychological Research in Chinese Societies* [本土心理学研究] (12).

Ramasamy, B., Yeung, M., & Laforet, S. (2012). China's outward foreign direct investment: Location choice and firm ownership. *Journal of World Business, 47*(1), 17–25.

Selmer, J. (2010). Expatriate cross-cultural training for China: View and experience of 'China Hands'. *Management Research View, 33*(1), 41–53.

Shen, J., & Edwards, V. (2004). Recruitment and selection in Chinese MNEs. *The International Journal of Human Resource Management, 15*(4–5), 814–835.

Shi, L., & Wang, L. (2013). The culture shock and cross-cultural adaptation of Chinese expatriates in international business contexts. *International Business Research, 7*(1), 23–33.

Su, C., Mitchell, R. K., & Sirgy, M. J. (2007). Enabling guanxi management in China: A hierarchical stakeholder model of effective guanxi. *Journal of Business Ethics, 71*(3), 301–319.

Takeuchi, R. (2010). A critical review of expatriate adjustment research through a multiple stakeholder view: Progress, emerging trends, and prospects. *Journal of Management, 36,* 1040–1064.

Tan, D., & Snell, R. S. (2002). The third eye: Exploring guanxi and relational morality in the workplace. *Journal of Business Ethics, 41*(4), 361–384.

Vanhonacker, W. R. (2004). Guanxi networks in China. *China Business Review, 3*(3), 48–53.

Wang, D., Feng, T., Freeman, S., Fan, D., & Zhu, C. J. (2014). Unpacking the "skill—cross-cultural competence" mechanisms: Empirical evidence from Chinese expatriate managers. *International Business Review, 23*(3), 530–541.

Wang, D., Freeman, S., & Zhu, C. J. (2013). Personality traits and cross-cultural competence of Chinese expatriate managers: A socio-analytic and institutional perspective. *International Journal of Human Resource Management, 24*(20), 3812–3830.

Wong, Y. H., & Chan, R. Y. (1999). Relationship marketing in China: Guanxi, favouritism and adaptation. *Journal of Business Ethics, 22*(2), 107–118.

Wong, Y. H., Leung, T. K. P., Hung, H., & Ngai, E. W. T. (2007). A model of guanxi development: Flexibility, commitment and capital exchange. *Total Quality Management and Business Excellence, 18*(8), 875–887.

Wood, E. D., & Mansour, B. E. (2010). Performance interventions that assist Chinese expatriates' adjustment and performance: Toward a conceptual approach. *Human Resource Development Review, 9*(2), 194–218.

Xin, K., & Pearce, J. L. (1996). Guanxi: Connections as substitutes for formal institutional support. *Academy of Management Journal, 39*(6), 1641–1658.

Yang, M. M. (2002). The resilience of guanxi and its new deployments: A critique of some new guanxi scholarship. *The China Quarterly, 170*(170), 459–476.

Yao, C. (2014). The impact of cultural dimensions on Chinese expatriates' career capital. *The International Journal of Human Resource Management, 25*(5), 609–630.

Yao, C., Arrowsmith, J., & Thorn, K. (2016). Exploring motivations in Chinese corporate expatriation through the lens of Confucianism. *Asia Pacific Journal of Human Resources, 54*(3), 312–331.

Yao, C., Thorn, K., & Doherty, N. (2014). Boundarylessness as a dynamic construct: The case of Chinese early career expatriates. *Career Development International, 19*(6), 683–699.

Yau, O. H. M., Lee, J. S. Y., Chow, R. P. M., Sin, L. Y. M., & Tse, A. C. B. (2000). Relationship marketing the Chinese way. *Business Horizons, 43*(1), 16–24.

Yeung, I. Y. M., & Tung, R. L. (1996). Achieving business success in Confucian societies: The importance of Guanxi (connections). *Organisational Dynamics, 25*(2), 54–65.

Yu, X. (2016). *From east to west: A phenomenological study of Mainland Chinese expatriates' international adjustment experiences in the U.S. workplace.* Retrieved from conservancy.umn.edu.

Zhang, D. (2017). *China becomes world's second-largest source of outward FDI: Report.* Retrieved from http://www.xinhuanet.com/english/2017-06/08/c_ 136350164.htm.

Zhang, M. (2016). *How China and the EU can boost investment.* Retrieved from https://www.weforum.org/agenda/2016/10/how-china-and-the-eu-can-boost-investment.

Zhong, Y., Zhu, C. J., & Zhang, M. M. (2015). The management of Chinese MNEs' expatriates. *Journal of Global Mobility: The Home of Expatriate Management Research, 3*(3), 289–302.

5

Cross-Cultural Guanxi Leadership

Abstract Several scholars have addressed the important need of Chinese business leadership study in the Chinese social-economic system. Nevertheless, along with rapid growth of globalization of Chinese multinational companies (MNCs), how Chinese business leadership could be exercised effectively in the West is under investigated in the literature. This chapter examines Chinese leadership in order to reveal the features of China's management system embedded deeply in its cultural–social–political environment. It explores how Chinese leaders could effectively influence in foreign branches by reviewing paternalistic leadership, international assignments (IAs) of Chinese expatriates, and discussing the cultural intelligence (CI). The aim, therefore, is to develop a conceptual framework of cross-cultural guanxi leadership and the model of cross-cultural guanxi practice.

Keywords Chinese expatriates · Paternalistic leadership · Cultural intelligence · Influencing · Cross-cultural guanxi leadership · Guanxi practice

B. X. Wang, *Guanxi in the Western Context*,
https://doi.org/10.1007/978-3-030-24001-1_5

Introduction

Over past four decades, Western leadership theories and skills have prevailed in China and globally. Becoming the world's second-largest economy along with rapid globalization of Chinese MNCs, it is the time to explore how Chinese leadership skill applies to the West. In the West, leadership study has been the subject of numerous books over the last century and new researches continue to increasingly emerge (van Maurik, 2001, p. 1). Maurik (2001) encapsulated four generations of the development of leadership thinking, which were defined as (1) trait theory, (2) behavioural theories, (3) contingency theories, and (4) transformational leadership theories. There are almost as many definitions of leadership as there are authors who have attempted to define the concept (Stogdill, 1974). Yukl (2002) concluded that leadership is the process of influencing others to understand and agree about what needs to be done and how it can be done effectively and the process of facilitating individual and collective efforts to accomplish the shared objectives.

Tsui, Wang, Xin, Zhang, and Fu (2004) noted that the current Chinese business leadership is shaped by multiple forces, including traditional values such as Confucianism and Daoism, communist ideologies, economic reform, and Western management theories and practices. Several studies (Chen & Chen, 2004; Farh & Cheng, 2000; Silin, 1976) suggested that paternalistic leadership (PL) dominates in Chinese business and is idiosyncratic comparing to Western leadership theories, which is defined as a style that combines strong discipline and authority with fatherly benevolence and moral integrity couched in a personalistic atmosphere. Influencing is the essence in the current Western leadership literature, and it explicates the equal relationship between leaders and followers in a fluid dynamic among subordinates, peers, and superiors. In contrast, guanxi practising is the core of Chinese business leadership as it is the key characteristic of PL, and it highlights the hierarchical relationship between guanxi holders.

This chapter examines Chinese business leadership in order to reveal the characteristics of Chinese expatriates' (CEs) leadership embedded deeply in its cultural–social–political environment. It explores how the Chinese business leadership emerged, evolved, and exercised by reviewing the construct of leadership in the Chinese context, understanding international assignments (IAs) of Chinese expatriates, and discussing the cultural intelligence (CI). Therefore, the aim is to develop a conceptual framework of the "Cross-cultural Guanxi Leadership Development".

Leader and Leadership in the Chinese Context

Despite the construct of leader and leadership has existed in China for millennia to describe the role of imperial rulers and senior officials, and the most admired political figures are respectively addressed "Ling Xiu" (领袖) originated from "Book of Jin" in the Tang dynasty (Fang, 579–648), which means "collar and sleeve" to analogize a great person to the most important part of the robe. However, the semantic "leader" and "leadership" are loanwords from the West, which are not included in the Chinese dictionary (辞海, Cihai, 1999). The Chinese word "leader" (Ling Dao, 领导) is the phono-semantic matching translation of the English version, which was introduced to China during the Westernization Movement in the 1920s.

Since 1949, along with implementation of communism ideology in mainland China, the word "leader" was mainly associated with the political position in the governments till 1980s, ever since, it has been prevailed in the SOEs as most of senior managers were transferred from the governments. Therefore, only the senior managers are addressed "leader" which is the synonyms for "boss" and the legitimated title granted by the organization. The concept of "leadership" was introduced to mainland China even later around 2000 when the Western management theories and practice have prevailed. The Chinese word "leadership" literally means "leading ability"; thus, it is believed only for the senior management to possess. Consequently, most Chinese people think that leader and leadership have nothing to do with the ordinary people.

In Chinese context, the word "leader" has a strong sense of hierarchy. What leaders do is to manage people, process, and resources, develop goals, and make decisions. Hence, everyone surrounds the leaders, hinges on the will of leaders, and achieves the goals of leaders. Unlike the Western termed leader and leadership according to transformational leadership theory which can be applied to anyone who has positive influence on others at workplace, the Chinese term of leader and leadership is only in relation to the senior managers and their leading competence. Given the borrowed word from the West, it is a bit "lost in translation" in the Chinese context.

According to the transformational leadership theory (Bass, 1990), whether a "Manager" assigned by the organization can be considered a "leader" is not determined by his/her position or organization, but by his/her subordinates or peers. If, in the process of leading the team, the manager makes great efforts to establish healthy interpersonal relationship, clarify the direction, build high-performing team, lift his/her team members to better their selves, unlock their potentials, and ultimately achieve the common goal of the team, this manager would become a leader. Leaders and leadership are given by followers. In other words, you can be considered a leader only if you have a follower, and a follower cannot be appointed and should come not only from subordinates but also from your peers and superiors. Therefore, there is no hierarchy between leader and follower, and if you have only subordinates, then you are just a manager. Being a CEO means you are a high-level professional manager, but does not automatically make you a leader, and you need to work hard to win the recognition as a leader.

In the West, those who win followers will become leaders, among whom there are not only politicians and entrepreneurs, but also ordinary civil servants, staff, and social workers, but without followers, no matter how high your position is, you are not a leader. In China, a leader is determined by the position printed on a business card. Therefore, when Westerners introduce their superiors, you usually hear "this is the CEO of our company", but rarely, "this is our leader", because the latter is a very high mark, which not only establishes the status of the leader, but also shows the admiration of the follower. In China, it is quite the opposite, and it often hears the introduction like "this is our leader".

In addition, there are tremendous differences in the role and function of leaders. In China, it is advocated that leaders should give subordinates direction, decisions, resources, and incentives, hoping them to be loyal, and have absolute authority and assume full responsibility. Leaders are lecturers, who know the answers and set an example by personally taking part, so leadership is reflected by the leaders and oriented by completing specific tasks.

In the West, it is advocated that leaders should fully share information with subordinates or followers, discuss the direction and make decisions together, seek resources together, give personalized incentives, conduct full debates, and seek common ground while reserving differences; leaders should delegate fully, and the team should share responsibility together. Leaders are catalysts and coaches, who do not necessarily know the answers, but help subordinates and followers find their own answers and complete the tasks in a way suitable for them, so leadership is reflected by the teams and oriented by focusing on the process of completing the tasks. Taking "Belbin's team roles" developed by Meredith Belbin (2010) as an example, he argued that a high-performing team needed six competencies including leadership and nine roles, in which there is no such role as a leader. Team members should take roles suitable for themselves according to their respective expertise. Each role can be the person in charge of the team and has the possibility to become a leader, but the "coordinator" and "shaper" among them are more likely to be the "leader", and they can play a leading role in the team, although not necessarily the "manager" of the team. But in China, if a team member who is not the manager demonstrating leadership, he/she might be suspected of exceeding his/her authority and even be removed from his/her position.

Leadership Style of Chinese Expatriates

In the literature on international business and management, the success of multinational corporations is frequently linked to the work of expatriates sent by headquarters to ensure the communication to subsidiaries (Harris & Kumra, 2000; Harzing, 2001). Ideally, this should be a two-way inter-action where both parties learn from each other (Brewster, 1995; Edström & Galbraith, 1977). Therefore, expatriation has often been viewed as an effective way to bridge communication and maintain knowledge sharing between the different parties in a multinational corporation (Bennett, Aston, & Colquhoun, 2000; Boyacigiller, 1990). However, as described in Chapter 4, unlike the expatriates from developed economy, Chinese expatriates from emerging Chinese MNCs possess their own characteristics. One of the challenges to CEs who comparatively have had less exposure to international businesses than their Western counterparts (Zheng, 2013). The leadership behaviours among CEs can be very different in terms of the two variables: (1) generation—most of CEs belong to "born in the 50s and 60s" (Cultural Revolution) and "born in the 70s" (Social Reform), which carry its own subculture respectively and (2) career experience—most of them are developed in state-owned enterprises (SOEs) and Chinese private companies in China, and few of them might be developed in foreign multinationals. Their leadership styles can be determined by Chinese business cultures.

Paternalistic Leadership (PL)

Farh and Cheng (2000) defined prominent Chinese business leadership as PL, which is a style that combines strong discipline and authority with fatherly benevolence and moral integrity couched in a personalistic style. PL is believed the dominating styles of Chinese senior managers (Barkema, Chen, George, Luo, & Tsui, 2011; Li & Scullion, 2010; Zhang, Chen, Chen, & Ang, 2014). PL consists of four characteristics:

1. Authoritarianism, absolute authority and control over subordinates and demands unquestionable obedience from subordinates. Thus, when the headquarters assign the task to overseas branches, which is normally the final decision for CEs to implement without further discussion. The expatriates are expected to allocate specific target to team members consisting of host-country nationals (HCNs) with one-way communication (Chen, Friedman, Yu, & Sun, 2011);
2. Benevolence, individualized, holistic concern for subordinates' personal, or familial well-being. Furthermore, the definition of individualized care subordinates in China goes beyond Western notions, which refers to the supervisor's care about the subordinate's work and career development (Bass, 1995). In Chinese context, individualized care means that the supervisor is expected to care about the employees' families and personal lives as well as their work and career; therefore,

life and work for the Chinese are much less distinctly separated (Cheng, Chou, Wu, Huang, & Farh, 2004; Zhang et al., 2014);

3. Moral leadership, superior personal virtues, self-discipline, and unselfishness. Chinese senior manager is expected to put work as priority before family and own welfare. Many expatriates working overseas branches live alone without taking their spouses and children, and they dedicate to work excessively overtime as they have the sense of obligation to the headquarters (Chen & Chen, 2004);

4. Guanxi-oriented, guanxi practice is the key skill to gain trust, establish better communication, and get things done. Most expatriates have IA opportunities through guanxi holders even though they are capable for their posts.

Chinese Leadership Challenge in the West

In their research, Ju, Xie, and Bao (2008) and Zhang et al. (2014) found that authoritarianism of PL is negatively related with employees' trust in supervisors, work attitudes, firm performance, and group creativity. Zhang et al. (2014) suggested that the effectiveness of leadership is contingent upon employees' value orientation. Needless to say, if the Chinese subordinates find their supervisors' authoritarianism difficult to take, it would be a real challenge for both CEs and the HCNs in the West, and this indicates that typical PL applied by CEs may not be suitable for meeting host-country expectations in foreign locations.

As latecomers of globalization, Chinese MNCs go abroad to cooperate and compete with enterprises from different countries. Like participating in a game played by Westerners for many years, CEs are smart and intelligent, with a strong learning ability, and have mastered some rules of the game, but they have suffered setbacks as they not only lacked actual international experience, but also understood the culture and value of HCNs in cognition of Chinese way, which would no doubt lead to misunderstanding of and contradictions with HCNs. In many cases, even though all parties wanted to succeed, they often broke up in the end. Just as the old English proverb says, the road to hell is paved with good intentions.

It is common for Chinese firms to request their staff to work overtime, paid or unpaid, in short notice. However, working overtime is discouraged in the West for legal, social, and cultural/religious reasons (Cooke, 2012). Some CEs tried to educate HCNs and give them reward and recognition. Nevertheless, asking a HCN to work overtime or discuss work through private WeChat outside of work time, she/he might bring a lawsuit for the infringement of privacy or personal rights. CEs might think that the Western world is lack of human touch, and HCNs are selfish, while HCNs might think that CEs breach the rules and violate laws and disciplines.

Criticizing subordinates might be very common in China, and it can be the end of career for a senior manager in the West, who might end up in court for misconduct of discrimination or dismissive. Therefore, Western companies tend to hew to the line in everything, while Chinese enterprises tend to understand and help each other. Thus, the Western concept of "rule of law" and the Chinese concept of "rule of man" are contradictory at all levels in the society, businesses, and daily work and life of individuals. This contradiction is invisible and imperceptible, and the two parties are usually unconscious to it and therefore think that the other party is unreasonable. This difference in the concept of thinking has also put some Chinese enterprises in a tricky situation in the process of globalization.

Wang, Feng, Freeman, Fan, and Zhu (2014) noted that due to the limited international experience and different managerial values practised in the home context, it is likely that CEs' ability is inadequate for overcoming lack of local knowledge and gaining trust from HCNs. Johnson, Lenartowicz, and Apud (2006) argued that there is a gap between "knowing" and "doing", where expatriates can understand host cultural expectations but may lack the leadership skill to influence them effectively. Johnson et al. (2006) believed that the way to work successfully with people from different national cultural backgrounds at home or abroad is in drawing upon a set of knowledge, skills, and personal attributes. Therefore, endeavouring on cultural intelligence will improve the influencing skills CEs to lead in host countries.

Cultural Intelligence (CQ)

The CQ is defined by Thomas (2008) as a system of interacting knowledge and skills, linked by cultural meta-cognition, which allows people to adapt to, select, and shape the cultural aspects of their environment. It needs to build adaptive skills and a repertoire of leadership behaviours in order to be effective in different intercultural situations. Alon, Boulanger, Meyers, and Taras (2016) noted that CQ includes international situations requiring cross-border leadership effectiveness.

Alon et al. (2016) concluded that although the CQ is a relatively new construct in international business research, it has the potential of becoming in international business and management what the emotional intelligence (EQ) has become in HR/OB/I-O Psychology. Alon and Higgins (2005) indicated that the CQ is not only associated with expatriate success, but also with the development of global leadership. Ang et al. (2007) developed four dimensions of CQ:

1. Metacognitive: higher-order thinking and involves mental processes used to understand cultural knowledge. It has been shown to predict situational cultural judgments, decision-making, and performance of tasks;
2. Cognitive: knowledge of norms, practices, and conventions in different cultures acquired from education and personal experiences and knowledge of basic frameworks for cultural values, such as those offered by Hofstede and McCrae (2004);
3. Motivational: capability to direct attention and energy towards learning about and functioning in situations that are characterized by cultural differences; and
4. Behavioural: the capability to exhibit appropriate verbal and non-verbal actions when interacting with people from different cultures.

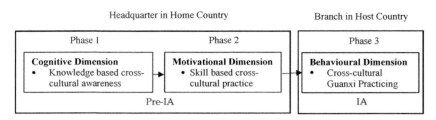

Fig. 5.1 Framework of cross-cultural guanxi leadership development

Cross-Cultural Guanxi Leadership Development

In their research, Fu and Yukl (2000) found that Western managers believed that influence aimed directly at the targeted person is more effective, whereas Chinese managers viewed guanxi practice through third party to be more effective given the Chinese culture of face-saving and harmony. Given that influencing is the most shared proposition of leadership in the West, it would be the beneficial for all parties in foreign branches of Chinese MNCs if CE is able to employ guanxi practice as an influencing tool. Based on the analysis of guanxi practice in early chapters, leadership characterizes of CEs and Chinese construct of leader and leadership, grounded on the PL and CI dimensions, the concept of cross-cultural guanxi leadership is developed and defined to influence others across cultures by guanxi practice. The framework of cross-cultural guanxi leadership development is illustrated in Fig. 5.1 to provide insight into Chinese MNCs to develop their expatriates for effectively leading foreign branches.

Pre-IAs Development

Cross-cultural guanxi leadership development is crucial to enable expatriates to influence effectively in the host country, the headquarter needs to play the key role in designing and leading development plan, and training programmes for expatriates, specifically, focus on (1) selecting candidate of IAs from the talent pool; (2) organizing internal and external recourses to deliver Phase 1&2 training programmes; (3) participating programmes to foreground the value and attitude in expatriates; and (4) providing clear strategy, objectives, and expectations for expatriate to lead in overseas branches.

Phase 1: Cognitive Dimension
In this stage, a series of classroom training aiming to raise knowledge-based cross-cultural awareness is to improve expatriates' cognitive ability in terms of cultural knowledge such as values, norms, artefacts, and practices of China and host countries. Help expatriates understand the cultural difference and distance between China and host countries, increase self-awareness of their own cultural values and behaviours, and then realize the need to respect and accept other cultures by leading differently from they are doing in China. Therefore, the outcome of Phase 1 is to answer the "what" question of cross-cultural influencing.

Phase 2: Motivational Dimension
In this phase, it is the skill-based cross-cultural practice. The expatriates need motivation to make efforts to stretch themselves out of the "comfort zone" and really experience the cultural difference, more importantly, gain confidence to live and lead in the alien culture. This can be a "prelude" of the IAs, and it might arrange expatriates to embark on three to six months "internship" or "live case" working in a multicultural project team as one of the team members, ideally, not in their own organizations. During this period, a mentor from the headquarter allocated to each expatriate for providing mental or moral support would motivate the expatriate to attain the positive attitude towards learning about and functioning in situations that are characterized by cultural differences. The outcome of Phase 2 is to answer the "why" question of cross-cultural influencing.

Development During IAs

Triandis (2012) summarized that cultural differences often lead to miscommunication, which can cause conflict. Merkin, Taras, and Steel (2014) noted that communication across cultures increasingly common in the globalization process, and understanding the sources of cross-cultural communication challenges is becoming a bigger issue. They further emphasized that assumptions about one's communication preferences based on one's cultural background must be made with caution and factors other than cultural values must be also taken into account. Western preconceptions of good communication are about clarity, which might be challenging for Chinese, Hall (1976) defined Chinese is high-context cultures, and there is a great deal of subtext. Communication depends on the context or non-verbal aspect of communication. In low-context cultures, such as most Western ones, communication depends more on explicit, expressed content, and has the following characteristics (Wang & Chee, 2011): (1) interpretation depends on what is actually said or written; (2) expertise and performance are valued above reputation or connections; (3) legal contracts are necessary and binding; and (4) personal relationships are not a priority.

Phase 3: Behavioural Dimension

This is the time to tackle the "how" question. Based on the learning from pre-IAs training, the expatriates are expected to show their capability of exhibiting appropriate verbal and non-verbal actions when interacting with HCNs and HCC from various cultures in branches. As discussed early in this chapter that the three characterizes of PL, i.e. authoritarianism, benevolence, morality, and guanxi practice are embedded in Chinese culture, it is important for CEs to adapt to the host-country culture by recognizing one's own culture. It might be a good theory to exercise Western leadership to adapt host-country culture, it won't be realistic and applicable given that the expatriates need to keep the Chinese way to constantly interact with the headquarter based in China, further, as growing out from the Chinese culture, and CEs are not able to switch their "culture" to another no matter consciously or unconsciously. Therefore, cross-cultural guanxi practising might be the effective way to influence people in the host countries. The outcome of Phase 3 is to answer the "how" question of cross-cultural influencing.

   Cross-cultural Guanxi Practising, the effective influencing in the host country includes appropriate and context-specific ways of initiating interactions with locals, carrying-on meaningful dialogue with HCNs, and clearing-up misinterpretation and misunderstanding in the host-country working environment. Expatriates need to understand that competence goes beyond understanding local expectations and mainly relies on effective influencing skills to enhance their competence in host operations and

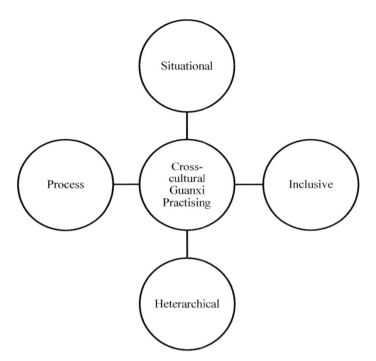

Fig. 5.2 Model of cross-cultural guanxi practising

management. In Chapter 3, despite guanxi practice has been exercised only between CEs given their homogeneous cultural background, HCNs and HCC have also expressed their intentions of being involved in guanxi practice. Therefore, CEs are suggested to initiate guanxi practising with local people to influence effectively. The model of cross-cultural guanxi practising illustrated in Fig. 5.2 provides the way to effectively influence others in the host country:

Situational. Guanxi practice involves people at both social and institutional environment, requiring both emotional and rational connection at personal level, which might make some non-Chinese feel uneasy. Hence, it depends on the situation when the counterpart is willing to engage this behaviour.

Inclusive. Typical guanxi practice is very exclusive to anyone out of inner circle, and guanxi holders and actors are closely interrelated with strong ties. In the cross-cultural context, guanxi holders need to break the boundary to include weak ties outside guanxi circle, which means that CEs need to initiate guanxi practice with local people including HCNs, HCC, and external business partners.

Heterarchical. As described in Chapter 2, typical guanxi practice is hierarchical depending on the influential power of guanxi holders. The Tier 1 guanxi holder has more privilege than other tiers. In the cross-cultural context of Western democratic culture, CEs need to be mindful of the cultural difference and sensitivity and interact with local people in an equal manner.

Process. As illustrated in Chapter 4, it takes time to develop guanxi involving a 4-stage process of initiation, building, utilization, and maintenance. Although it is time-consuming, it is rewarding as it might be the effective influencing approach to motivate and lead multicultural team in the host country.

Here are some points for cross-cultural guanxi practising:

- Share important information with team first and then conduct private conversation with each team member;
- Use common language in a workplace, in particular in meetings;
- Interact as a coach; show sincerity and an open mind, listen first, then talk, give, and take non-judgemental feedback, be specific and precise; show your interest and support in others' ideas, check misunderstanding. "So what you're saying is…"
- Take team out for retreat or team building activities;
- Celebrate success openly and give private recognition;
- Organize team party inviting their family member for important public holidays;
- Treat all people equally at workplace.

Discussion and Conclusion

Professor Joseph Nye (2004) of Harvard University proposed the concept of "soft power" in 1980, which means the ability to attract and influence others or other countries. The influence of a country's culture on other countries best reflects its soft power. However, hard power is a mandatory capability, such as the use of force and money. Soft power is built on hard power, and without hard power, there will be no soft power; but having hard power does not mean the possession of soft power. Chinese MNCs' hard power has been increased enormously with outward investment in the West; however, the soft power reflected by CEs, leadership with effective influencing, is still behind the successful Western MNCs.

From the beginning of globalization to date, the home countries of globalized Western enterprises have often been developed countries, which means that their hard power (monetary and technology) and soft power (management philosophy and leadership skills) are both very strong. However, the host countries have mostly been developing countries, of which the hard power is unsatisfactory, not to mention the soft power. Therefore, the bases of globalization of Western companies are leading technologies and products as well as effective management tools and leadership skills. They mainly seek labour force and markets and pursue long-term returns in host countries, with clear and sound strategies. In particular, they achieve cooperation and win-win situation with host countries through the leadership of their home countries. That is why most of the host countries admire them and are friendly and respectful to them. Employees who are able to work in Western companies not only earn more than those in domestic enterprises, but also enjoy an enviable social position. Therefore, Western companies may have some challenges in individual business management in the process of globalization, but they are accepted and looked up at the social level of host countries.

China is a developing country, of which the hard power may have reached a certain level that attracts world attention, but the leadership influencing is far behind that of developed countries. Portland Company of UK created a global ranking of soft power since 2015, which was mainly based on the cultural influence of a country on other countries. The research result showed that only 30 countries in the world had various levels of cultural influence on other countries. China was at the bottom of the list in 2015, and ranked 28th in 2016, 25th in 2017, and at the bottom of the list in 2018 again (Mcclory, 2018), sharp contrast to its ranking as the world's second-largest economy. Even if compared with Asian countries, China still behind Japan, Singapore, and Korea.

Chinese people might think that this is a Western standard, but globalization is a game invented by the West. Chinese MNCs are only players of the game, and the rules of the game are still Western standards. Since Chinese MNCs have decided to participate in it, they need to understand and follow these standards to survive and strive. A relatively smooth path of globalization is paved with the strong soft power of the home country as the cornerstone.

It can be seen that the globalization of Chinese MNCs can be described as rowing against the current. Compared with Western companies, the purpose of the globalization of many Chinese MNCs is to seek the most fundamental resources and technologies for the survival of enterprises and to pursue short-term returns, which might lead to unclear strategies and blind decision-making. Due to the weak influence of Chinese culture on host countries, HCNs hold diversified attitudes towards Chinese enterprises. Therefore, Chinese MNCs need to make more efforts and pay more costs than Western companies if they want to develop in host countries.

As China's leadership influencing is not strong enough, Chinese MNCs should be cautious about globalization. They need to have financial strength, but more importantly, they should enhance their own influencing skills by benchmarking with well-received enterprises in developed countries and developing expatriates who understand and accept the culture of host countries, as well as their own country and organization.

The Western society advocates individualism and that personal interests are above everything else. This is also reflected in business administration, and Western enterprises try to satisfy personal interests of employees from CEO to a cleaner as much as possible. Western companies understand and accept individual differences, which is based on cognition of human nature in Western modern psychology. Therefore, even if Western companies operate in host countries with significantly different ideology, such as China, Japan, and the Middle East, they can also accept and respect the personalities and working styles of local employees. So Chinese employees working in foreign companies have more individuality and freedom, but they also need to be self-reliant and independent.

China is a family-centric country, where national interests are above everything else and family interests higher than personal interests, so business interests are higher than those of employees. Chinese enterprises expect employees to regard enterprises as their family, which means that employees are expected to sacrifice personal interests when needed. Taking overtime, the most common phenomenon, as an example, Chinese enterprises do not think it a personal sacrifice and are even proud of it; while in many Western countries, individual family comes first, and over time not only reflects low efficiency, but also is employees' sacrifice of personal interests and disrespect for their families. If Chinese MNCs put forward the same requirement on employees of host countries, the conflict may be self-evident. One of the key elements for the success of globalization is the international talent pool, which is often diversified and individualized. The twenty-first century is a century of talent competition, and international talents are also the goal of all enterprises and probably cannot be replaced by artificial intelligence. If Chinese MNCs cannot protect the personal interests of employees according to Western standards, it would be difficult for them to attract international talents.

In conclusion, the path of globalization of Chinese MNCs has been more difficult than that of Western MNCs from the very beginning. It seems that "all roads lead to Rome", but every road is often a dead end. Whether to follow the footsteps of Western companies or explore a different track depends on how influential CEs can be in the host country. Since the rules of the game of globalization were developed by Western companies, it would be wise for CEs to enhance influencing power through cross-cultural guanxi practising which integrates best practice from both Chinese and Western cultures.

References

Alon, I., Boulanger, M., Meyers, J., & Taras, V. (2016). The development and validation of the business cultural intelligence quotient. *Cross Cultural & Strategic Management, 23*(1), 78–100.

Alon, I., & Higgins, J. M. (2005). Global leadership success through emotional and cultural intelligences. *Business Horizons, 48,* 501–512.

Ang, S., Van Dyne, L., Koh, C., Ng, K. Y., Templer, K. J., Tay, C., & Chandrasekar, N. A. (2007). Cultural intelligence: Its measurement and effects on cultural judgment and decision making, cultural adaptation and task performance. *Management and Organization Review, 3*(3), 335–371.

Barkema, H., Chen, X.-P., George, G., Luo, Y., & Tsui, A. (2011). West meets East: New concepts and theories. *Academy of Management Journal, 54*(3), 642–644.

Bass, B. M. (1990). *Bass & Stogdill's handbook of leadership* (3rd ed.). New York: The Free Press.

Bass, B. M. (1995). Theory of transformational leadership redux. *Leadership Quarterly, 6*(4), 463–478.

Belbin, R. (2010). *Team roles at work* (2nd ed.). London: Routledge.

Bennett, R., Aston, A., & Colquhoun, T. (2000). Cross-cultural training: A critical step in ensuring the success of international assignments. *Human Resource Management, 39*(2), 239–250.

Boyacigiller, N. (1990). The role of expatriates in the management of interdependence, complexity and risk in multinational corporations. *Journal of International Business Studies, 21*(3), 357–381.

Brewster, C. (1995). Effective expatriate training. In J. Selmer (Ed.), *Expatriate management: New ideas for international business* (pp. 57–71). Westport, CT: Quorum Books.

Chen, X.-P., & Chen, C. C. (2004). On the intricacies of the Chinese guanxi: A process model of guanxi development. *Asia Pacific Journal of Management, 21*(3), 305–324.

Chen, Y., Friedman, R., Yu, E., & Sun, F. (2011). Examining the positive and negative effects of guanxi practices: A multi-level analysis of guanxi practices and procedural justice perceptions. *Asia Pacific Journal of Management, 28*(4), 715–735.

Cheng, B. S., Chou, L. F., Wu, T. Y., Huang, M. P., & Farh, J. L. (2004). Paternalistic leadership and subordinate responses: Establishing a leadership model in Chinese organizations. *Asian Journal of Social Psychology, 7*(1), 89–117.

Cihai. (1999). *Chinese dictionary and encyclopedia.* The Zhonghua Book Company, Shanghai Lexicographical Publishing House.

Cooke, F. L. (2012). The globalisation of Chinese telecom corporations: Strategy, challenges and HR implications for the MNCs and host countries. *The International Journal of Human Resource Management, 23*(9), 1832–1852.

Edström, A., & Galbraith, J. R. (1977). Transfers of managers as a coordination and control strategy in multinational organizations. *Administrative Science Quarterly, 22,* 248–263.

Fang, X. (648). *Book of Jin.* China: Tang Dynasty.

Farh, J. L., & Cheng, B. S. (2000). A cultural analysis of paternalistic leadership in Chinese organizations. In J. T. Li, A. S. Tsui, & E. Weldon (Eds.), *Management and organizations in the Chinese context* (pp. 84–130). London: Macmillan.

Fu, P. P., & Yukl, G. (2000). Perceived effectiveness of influence tactics in the United States and China. *Leadership Quarterly, 11,* 251–266.

Hall, D. T. (1976). *Careers in organizations.* Pacific Palisades, CA: Goodyear.

Harris, H., & Kumra, S. (2000). International manager development: Cross-cultural training in highly diverse environments. *Journal of Management Development, 19*(7), 602–614.

Harzing, A. W. K. (2001, Summer). Who is in charge: An empirical study of executive staffing practices in foreign subsidiaries. *Human Resource Management, 40*(2), 139–158.

Hofstede, G., & McCrae, R. (2004). Personality and culture revisited: Linking traits and dimensions of culture. *Cross-Cultural Research, 38*(1), 52–88.

Johnson, J. P., Lenartowicz, T., & Apud, S. (2006). Cross-cultural competence in international business: Toward a definition and a model. *Journal of International Business Studies, 37*(4), 525–543.

Ju, F., Xie, Z., & Bao, G. (2008). Western countries and China: A comparative study on the effects of the paternalistic leadership and transformational leadership on the performance of private enterprises. *Management World, 5,* 85–101. (In Chinese.)

Li, S., & Scullion, H. (2010). Developing the local competence of expatriate managers for emerging markets: A knowledge-based approach. *Journal of World Business, 45,* 190–196.

Mcclory, J. (2018). *A global ranking of soft power—The soft power 30.* Portland.

Merkin, R., Taras, V., & Steel, P. (2014). State of the art themes in cross-cultural communication research: A systematic and meta-analytic review. *International Journal of Intercultural Relations, 38*(1), 1–23.

Nye, J. S., Jr. (2004) *Soft power: The means to success in world politics.* New York: Public Affairs.

Silin, R. H. (1976). *Leadership and value: The organization of large-scale Taiwan enterprises.* Cambridge, MA: Harvard University Press.

Stogdill, R. M. (1974). *Handbook of leadership.* New York: The Free Press.

Thomas, D. C. (2008). *Cross-cultural management: Essential concepts.* Thousand Oaks, CA: Sage.

Triandis, H. C. (2012). Culture and conflict. In L. A. Samovar, R. E. Porter, & E. R. McDaniel (Eds.), *Intercultural communication: A reader* (13th ed., 10, pp. 34–44). Boston, MA: Wadsworth.

Tsui, A. S., Wang, H., Xin, K., Zhang, L., & Fu, P. P. (2004). "Let a thousand flowers bloom": Variation of leadership styles among Chinese CEOs. *Organizational Dynamics, 33*(1), 5–20.

van Maurik, J. (2001). *Writers on leadership.* London, UK: Penguin Books.

Wang, B. X., & Chee, H. (2011). *Chinese leadership.* Basingstoke: Palgrave Macmillan.

Wang, D., Feng, T., Freeman, S., Fan, D., & Zhu, C. J. (2014). Unpacking the "skill—cross-cultural competence" mechanisms: Empirical evidence from Chinese expatriate managers. *International Business Review, 23*(3), 530–541.

Yukl, G. (2002). *Leadership in organizations* (5th ed.). Upper Saddle River, NJ: Prentice-Hall International Inc.

Zhang, Z. X., Chen, (George) Z. X., Chen, Y. R., & Ang, S. (2014). Business leadership in the Chinese context: Trends, findings, and implications. *Management and Organization Review, 10*(2), 199–221.

Zheng, C. (2013). Critiques and extension of strategic international human resource management framework for dragon multinationals. *Asia Pacific Business Review, 19*(1), 1–15.

6

Conclusion

Abstract This chapter summarizes the entire book focusing on key research findings, managerial implication and limitation, and future research. It argues the contribution to the field of guanxi and social network theory in the cross-cultural context and highlights six models and frameworks developed in this book and their impact and importance.

Keywords Managerial implication · Future research · Chinese code

It is not surprising that Western host country nationals (HCNs) have reacted strongly to the speed of China's unprecedented economic rise, especially given the contrast between Chinese culture and institutions and Western systems. The concept of business in China is not the same as it is in the West, and, to some extent, maintaining good guanxi is paramount for personal welfare and business prosperity for Chinese people, with blurred boundaries between business, politics, and social life. Confucian values, such as guanxi, hierarchy, and harmony, determine the behavioural patterns of people working in Chinese multinational companies (MNCs). As Hammond and Glenn (2004, p. 29) concluded, it "is a

© The Author(s) 2019
B. X. Wang, *Guanxi in the Western Context*,
https://doi.org/10.1007/978-3-030-24001-1_6

naïve perspective" to suppose that "forces of globalisation will eliminate the need for guanxi".

In my book, I have achieved my research goal of understanding how the employees of Chinese MNCs employ guanxi in the West, how the practice of guanxi affects multicultural group dynamics, how Chinese expatriates (CEs) develop guanxi in their host countries, and how these behaviours affect their adjustment. I conducted total 71 semi-structured in-depth interviews (including Chapters 3 and 4) with informants representing three cultural clusters (mainland Chinese, HCC, and HCN) based in seven European countries, France, Germany, Luxemburg, the Netherlands, Portugal, Sweden, and the UK, thus studying a range of cultural and institutional contexts in the West.

The key findings of my study are the following.

First, at the intra-firm level, CEs actively practice guanxi with their homeland counterparts, but they do not do so with HCNs and Host country Chinese (HCC). The practice of guanxi, therefore, fosters the cohesion of the CE group and merges the HCC and HCN groups, but it enlarges the social distance between the two Chinese groups, the CE group, and the HCC group. Second, at the extra-firm level, CEs tend to make an effort to develop guanxi with both HCNs and HCC, which significantly alters their adjustment curve.

In particular, the findings reported in Chapter 3 indicate that intra-firm guanxi practices by CEs have a strong impact on group dynamics in the host country. Most CEs are not aware of the unspoken or unconscious needs of HCC and HCNs to participate in guanxi practices, and, in contrast, CEs assume that HCC and HCNs are ambivalent towards guanxi. CEs' detachment from guanxi practices with their host-country peers has a negative effect on intra-firm group dynamics and ethics.

The findings reported in Chapter 4 suggest that the process of the development of extra-firm guanxi significantly affects the adjustment of CEs, making their honeymoon stage much longer than that of their Western counterparts; in particular, the culture shock often occurs at the "moment of truth" when a return on investment by utilizing guanxi is expected. However, most Chinese MNCs and CEs are misled by the longer honeymoon stage because of the time-consuming nature of the initiation and building of guanxi; hence, they are not aware of the great cultural differences while interacting with Westerners.

My findings contribute to social network theory in the cross-cultural context, as mine is one of the first studies to offer insights from data from Chinese SOEs expanding into developed markets. The investigation extends the theory by proposing: (1) a model of guanxi practice affecting group dynamics, detailing in-/out-group activation, allowing multinational firms to overcome the in-/out-group barriers arising from the misuse of guanxi and ultimately to build high-performing teams in host countries; (2) a process model for the development of guanxi from the perspective of the adjustment of CEs in Europe and the V-curve adjustment, taking into account contextualised constructs like culture shock and degree of adjustment; (3) a framework of cross-cultural guanxi leadership development, suggesting three-phase development for CEs in the period of pre-IA and IA from cognitive dimension, motivational dimension, and behavioural dimension; and (4) a model of cross-cultural guanxi practising, exposing four features to be applied in the Western context: (1) situational, (2) inclusive, (3) heterarchical, and (4) process.

This book also expands the stream of research on guanxi in particular, and social network ties in general. It investigates the role of guanxi in the globalization of Chinese firms within developed economies. Hence, the research offers a first step in a dynamic view of a concept that results from Chinese culture but has been brought into the modern business environment. The findings provide insights into which elements of guanxi are transferable to the business networks of developed markets, by illustrating a framework and models for their impact and importance.

Bian (2017) emphasized the significance of guanxi and its tacit nature, rooted in Confucian culture. He also echoed the late Chinese sociologist and anthropologist Fei Xiaotong, who held that studying and discussing guanxi in Chinese culture provides an invaluable opportunity for the next generation of Chinese scholars to contribute to international sociology. This book specifically studies guanxi in the Western social context, contributing to the accumulation of knowledge in this field. Bian (2017, p. 264) also raised questions such as these: "Under what institutional conditions do 'Chinese-ised' guanxi networks and 'westernised' structural-hole networks coexist in China? What role does each of these types of networks play in the social and organisational lives of both Chinese and non-Chinese organisations?".

The findings of this book provide some answers to these questions. I show that there is a coexistence of Chinese guanxi and Western social networks in Chinese MNCs operating in the West, with Chinese organizational culture being brought by CEs into the Western social domain, and Western social behaviour being foregrounded by HCNs, although this takes place outside rather than inside China. The role of guanxi is paradoxical. It helps CEs enormously in maintaining a sense of security and the coherence of the CE group when they are away from their home country, and in building long-term relationships with HCNs outside work for mutual benefit. On the other hand, it creates a distance between CEs and HCC, which lessens the motivation for HCC to work for Chinese MNCs, as well as reducing their loyalty. It also misleads CEs by prolonging their honeymoon stage of adjustment, which causes a deeper level of culture shock. The key role of networks in Chinese organizations operating in the West is primarily positive, which creates coherence between HCNs and HCC in the workplace.

Managerial Implications

The models developed in this research explain how it was possible for managers from China to enter developed markets successfully and to establish effective relationships and international assignments (IAs) in developed countries. The model for how the practice of guanxi affects intra-firm group dynamics suggests that Chinese firms may create cohesion within multicultural groups and build high-performance teams through the practice of guanxi not only by CEs but also by members of the HCC and HCN groups. However, this process requires two things: (1) CEs themselves need to go through an adjustment process for building guanxi in the developed country and (2) there must be a focus on building cognitive and affect-based trust as well as positive commitment. As a result, an emerging market SOE expanding to a developed country should deliberately consider those requirements with respect to its human resource recruitment and cross-cultural talent development strategies.

The process model for the development and adjustment of guanxi by CEs gives detail on the process of building guanxi and contrasts the approach in Western countries to the familiar Chinese guanxi-building process. To initiate business in developed markets CEs should first focus on building cognitive trust through cross-cultural competence, professionalism and open communications that consistently exceed the expectations of their Western counterparts. At a later stage, the focus should shift to building affective trust and positive commitment. This may be achieved by stressing long-term mutual benefits and focusing on the development of guanxi with key stakeholders. Having established a positive guanxi culture, CEs can access the business network in the developed country.

The framework of cross-cultural guanxi leadership development helps Chinese MNCs establish effective IA programmes for expatriate development, and the model of cross-cultural guanxi practising provides an effective influencing tool for CEs to lead multicultural teams in the host country.

In particular, Chinese SOEs striving to achieve competitive advantage in global markets need to understand the dynamics and differences in guanxi building when they are expanding overseas. The ability to build and manage guanxi in different parts of the world is critical for the success of SOEs. They must learn how to form their international strategies in terms of cross-cultural management and human resources management, according to the changing requirements of developed markets.

Limitations and Future Research

The theoretical insights from this book, as well as its limitations, suggest some fruitful directions for future research. All CE informants in this study had only worked for SOEs in China. The model of the development and adjustment of guanxi by CEs argues that the practice and building of guanxi may improve the sense of belonging for HCC and mitigate the culture shock of expatriate adjustment. Building on this, future research should look specifically at CEs from non-SOE firms and examine whether and how they build and adjust guanxi when working in developed countries.

In terms of methodology, a quantitative approach would be useful to test the models developed in this book. The model of how the practice of guanxi affects group dynamics can be tested in the institutional domain, which is task-driven, and the social domain, which is relationship-driven. The V-curve model can be tested through questionnaires and surveys. This approach may also be combined with one that investigates different settings from those considered here. For example, guanxi dynamics can be examined in other developed markets such as the USA.

Chen, Chen, and Huang (2013, p. 199) hoped that "guanxi theories and research would not only help illuminate the complexity of guanxi in Chinese organizations and societies but also that of human relations in the rest of the world". This book has explored guanxi from the perspective of the rest of the world, particularly shedding light on two under-investigated territories (Chen et al., 2013): (1) How dyadic intergroup guanxi practices affect multicultural work-group dynamics and (2) the empirical evidence for the process model of guanxi, which previously was largely conceptualized.

Dr Clotaire Rapaille (2006) developed the following national code:

The English code for England is CLASS,
The French code for France is IDEA,
The American code for the USA is DREAM,
The German code for Germany is ORDER.

I would like to take the liberty of suggesting to that, in his next edition of The Culture Code, **the Chinese code for China should be Guanxi!**

References

Bian, Y. (2017). The comparative significance of guanxi. *Management and Organisation Review, 13*(02), 261–267.

Chen, C. C., Chen, X.-P., & Huang, S. (2013). Chinese guanxi: An integrative review and new directions for future research [中国人的关系: 综合文献回顾及未来研究方向]. *Management and Organisation Review, 9*(1), 167–207.

Hammond, S. C., & Glenn, L. M. (2004). The ancient practice of Chinese social networking: Guanxi and social network theory. *Emergence: Complexity and Organisation, 6* (1–2), 24–31.

Rapaille, C. (2006). *The culture code.* New York, NY: Crown Publishing Group.

Index